SAME PAGE PARENTING

Align with Your Partner to Raise Happy, Confident & Resilient Kids

Martina Nova
MCP, RCC

Published in 2026 by
ULYSSES PRESS
an imprint of The Stable Book Group
32 Court Street, Suite 2109
Brooklyn, NY 11201
www.ulyssespress.com

Library of Congress Control Number: 2025944349
ISBN: 978-1-64604-858-8
eISBN: 978-1-64604-859-5

Acquisitions editor: Claire Sielaff
Managing editor: Claire Chun
Project editor: Renee Rutledge
Copy editor: Jan Hughes
Creative director: Iain Morris
Book design: Abbey Gregory
Artwork from shutterstock.com: cover hands © irasophiass, personal note pen © farmaninfirm, growth icons © matsabe

Printed in the United States
10 9 8 7 6 5 4 3 2 1

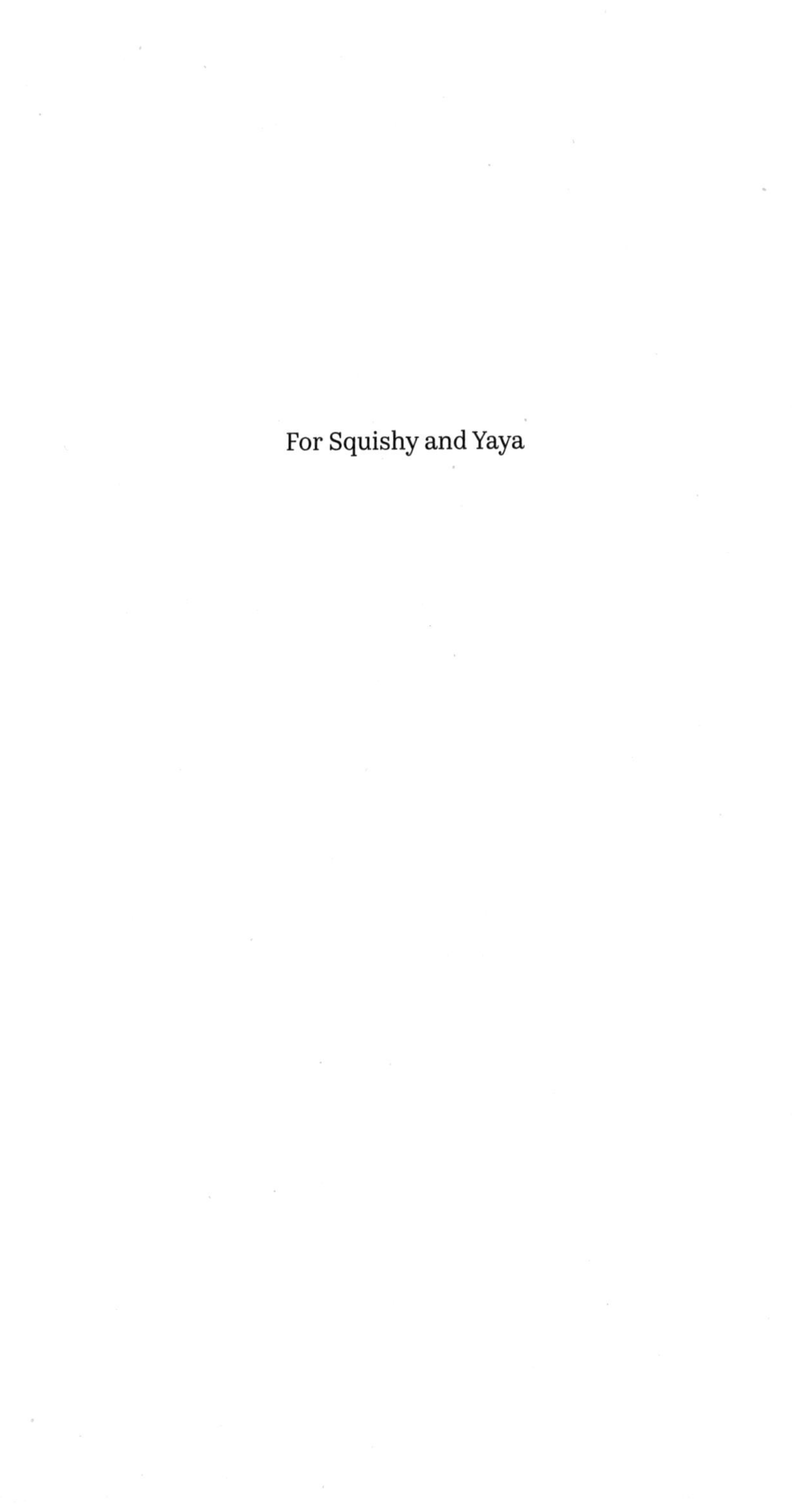

For Squishy and Yaya

CONTENTS

INTRODUCTION

Thank you for picking up this book and inviting it into your parenting journey. Whether you're just beginning to imagine life as a parent, navigating the thick of raising young children, or reflecting on your role with teenagers or adult children, I'm so glad you're here.

Parenting has a way of reshaping how we see ourselves, our relationships, and the world around us. It cracks things open in ways we don't always expect. We're the first generation raising children in a world of smartphones, social media, and constant connection, while also learning how to talk more openly about mental health, unlearn outdated roles, and break patterns we may have grown up with. It's a lot. And if you've ever wondered whether you're the only one trying to hold it all together, I want you to know that you're not.

Why I Wrote This Book

I'm Martina, a mother of two, a co-parent, a sister, a human being, and a trauma therapist based in Vancouver, BC. My passion lies in supporting individuals and couples through some of life's messier complexities: anxiety, relationships, neurodivergency, people-pleasing, motherhood, communication, and trauma, to name a few. This is my second book, following the release of a therapy journal, and it felt like the natural next step to go deeper into the parts of parenthood that often remain unspoken. My goal here is to offer guidance, practical tools, and, maybe most importantly, reassurance along the way.

As a first-generation Canadian, born in Slovakia and raised in Canada since I was one, I've come to deeply appreciate the blend of cultures and expectations that shape how we parent. Growing up in an immigrant family taught me about resilience, the value of community, and the quiet ways culture informs our roles, responsibilities, and emotional landscapes. Those experiences, combined with over a decade working in the health-care field, have shaped how I view the pressures that modern parents face, especially the ones no one really prepares you for.

In my clinical work, I've witnessed how people carry so much silently: burnout, emotional disconnection, resentment, fear of getting it wrong. And I've noticed something that's stuck with me: Often, the moments when things start to feel more manageable are the ones when we stop pushing forward alone and instead start talking with our partners, friends, family, community, and support networks. Sometimes it's a conversation that reveals where our rigidity or reactivity comes from. Sometimes it's simply naming that things feel hard and letting that be enough. This book is my way of making space for those conversations. These aren't prompts to get "the right answer"; they're invitations to pause, reflect, and connect.

What This Book Covers

This book is for anyone trying to raise children with intention and care, no matter what stage of parenting you're in. Maybe you're preparing for a baby, in the blur of toddlerhood, figuring out how to navigate big emotions in your child, or staying connected to your adult kids. Wherever you are, these reflections are here to meet you.

Each chapter explores a theme, such as boundaries with family, gender roles, the mental load, screen time, intimacy, financial values, consent, discipline, and trauma. You'll find thoughtful reflection questions broken down by life stage: pre-child, pregnancy, postpartum, 0–1 year, toddler years, 4–8 years, 9–12 years, teenagers, and adult children. We'll talk about reclaiming your voice amid family and cultural expectations, reimagining partnership roles, and navigating mental health after having a baby. We'll explore the ways your past influences your parenting, how to approach challenges with more self-awareness and kindness, and how to regain your footing after conflict or disconnection. We'll also delve into practical topics, including how to raise socially conscious kids, teach consent and safety, navigate emotionally complex holidays, and parent when you or your child is neurodivergent. You don't need to take it all in at once. Flip to what speaks to you right now and come back to the rest later.

Wisdom Acknowledgment

I want to acknowledge that this book wasn't written in isolation. It stands on the shoulders of so many brilliant minds—researchers, therapists, clients, friends, family members, parents, educators, authors, and advocates—whose insights, work, and lived experiences have helped shape the conversations we're finally having today.

These pages were born from the kinds of conversations that sneak into everyday life—quiet, honest, often unfinished. Some began in therapy sessions with clients working through the weight of parenting and partnership. Others came late at night, whispered through the fatigue of the day. To be honest, some are even questions

I wish my former husband and I asked one another, but we never knew how important it would have been to do so before certain issues arose in our relationship. Many arrived through voice notes exchanged with girlfriends while holding a baby in one arm and a cold coffee in the other. What they all had in common was a shared sense of wondering: *Are we doing this right? Why is this so hard? What are we allowed to want as parents, as people?*

The reflections and questions explored here are stitched together from those very moments—real stories, real struggles, real insight. They're shaped by what I've seen in my therapy practice, what I've lived in my own home, and what I've heard in parenting circles and support groups. They're also informed by the work of researchers, educators, and advocates who have dared to question traditional parenting norms, gender roles, and emotional labor, and offered new, more compassionate ways forward.

I'm deeply grateful to them, and to the clients, friends, and loved ones who continue to show me how much is possible when we make space for honest dialogue. Their wisdom, courage, and willingness to speak the unspeakable are woven into every part of this book. My hope is that it helps spark similar conversations in your own life, whether with a partner, a friend, a parent, a family member, or within your community.

A Note on Inclusivity

As you read through this book, you might find that certain topics bring up strong emotions or touch on tender parts of your story. All I ask is that you take a moment to reflect on this with curiosity and care for all parts of yourself. Some sections in this book mention conversations with a partner, but this book is not just for couples. You might be parenting solo, co-parenting across households, or raising a child with the help of extended family, close friends, or chosen community. You might be a biological parent, adoptive parent, foster parent, stepparent, or caregiver in another form. Whatever your family looks like, this book was written for you.

I also want to be transparent in pointing out that much of the framework in this book is shaped by a Western, individualistic lens. Having the time and space to reflect on parenting is a privilege. Many of our parents, and their parents before them, were doing their best under challenging circumstances, navigating immigration, systemic barriers, trauma, poverty, or simply trying to survive. These reflections might not take into consideration every reader's context or cultural framework, and that's important. Please feel free to adapt, question, or reshape anything here in a way that honors your lived experience.

How to Use This Book

This book is meant to be easy to pick up whenever you need it. Each chapter is broken into short sections with a mix of personal stories, context, reflection questions, and practical ideas. You don't have to read the topics in order; start wherever makes the most sense for you. While conversation starters in each subtopic are organized by a child's age, you might find questions in another section that feel more relevant to what you're experiencing right now. Maybe something from the toddler years still lingers in your relationship with your eight-year-old, or you're thinking ahead to what might come later. That's okay. Flip back or skip ahead. Use whatever pieces feel helpful, and leave the rest for another time.

Here are a few ways you might use this book:

* **Personal Reflection:** Use the questions as gentle prompts to dig deeper into your thoughts and emotions. Think of it like a guided heart-to-heart with yourself—no pressure, just a chance to listen in. Feel free to write down your answers in your journal or diary.
* **Relationship Conversation Starters:** Share some of the questions with your partner, community, or loved ones if that feels right for you, as a way to deepen your connection and explore the complexities of parenting together.
* **Therapy Tool:** Bring the ideas from this book into therapy, whether individually or with your partner. They can serve as a jumping-off point for deeper exploration.
* **Group Discussions:** Use these topics as conversation starters with friends, family, or parenting groups. Sometimes, sharing these experiences with others can shed light on how we all have unspoken shared experiences and can learn from one another.

A Personal Note: From a Parent and Therapist

I've lived many of these questions myself. I've had weeks where I felt like I was failing at everything—my work, my relationship, my parenting—and other moments where I felt grounded and proud. I've had messy talks with my ex-husband, breakdowns in the middle of bedtime routines, and voice notes from friends that reminded me I'm not alone.

This book reflects all of that. It's not meant to be a guide with all the answers (because I still have no idea what I'm doing half of the time). Instead, look at it as a gentle invitation to pause, notice what's coming up for you, and keep returning to what matters most. So, if you're reading this while tired, overwhelmed, or just needing something that feels like a soft place to land, you're in the right place. I'm walking alongside you. Let's figure it out together.

Chapter 1

RECLAIMING YOUR VOICE AS A PARENT

Parenting is one of the few life experiences that invites endless advice and unsolicited opinions, from family and friends to influencers on social media, strangers on the internet, and even well-meaning passersby at the grocery store. Everyone seems to have a viewpoint on how to handle tantrums, manage bedtime routines, or decide what your child should wear or eat. In this overwhelming sea of input, it's easy to lose touch with your instincts, feeling as though there's a "right" way to do everything, and that you're falling short if you deviate.

Reclaiming your voice as a parent is about stepping out of this noise and finding clarity in your values, instincts, and choices. It means creating a parenting style that works for your unique family dynamic, respecting both your child's needs and your own. Far from rejecting advice altogether, this process empowers you to filter out what doesn't align with your priorities, holding onto what resonates and discarding what doesn't.

The Psychology of Parenting Confidence

Understanding the psychological challenges of modern parenting reveals why reclaiming your voice is so crucial. Parents today face unprecedented pressures, amplified by the visibility of their decisions on social media and the sheer volume of conflicting advice from various sources. Studies show that when parents receive excessive or contradictory advice, it activates stress responses in the brain, leading to increased self-doubt, heightened anxiety, and a diminished ability to make decisions confidently.

Internalized expectations further compound this effect, a concept in psychology that refers to beliefs and standards we unconsciously absorb from our upbringing, culture, and societal norms. These expectations can create a cognitive dissonance between how we feel compelled to parent and how we intuitively want to parent. For example, if you grew up in a household that emphasized strict discipline but find yourself drawn to a gentler, more collaborative approach, you might feel torn or uncertain about whether you're doing the "right" thing.

Parenting confidence doesn't mean knowing all the answers. It means trusting your ability to make decisions that are attuned to your child's unique needs and to navigate the challenges with resilience. Reclaiming this confidence requires self-reflection, intentionality, and a willingness to challenge deeply ingrained societal and personal expectations.

Why Reclaiming Your Voice Matters

When parents operate from a place of confidence and self-trust, it fosters emotional security for both them and their children. Research in attachment theory shows that when parents feel emotionally stable and supported in their decisions, they are better equipped to meet their children's needs for connection, autonomy, and boundaries. Conversely, when parents are consumed by doubt or external validation, it can create inconsistency and anxiety in family dynamics.

By reclaiming your voice, you give your child the gift of modeling self-assurance and authenticity. You show them what it means to honor your values and to approach life with curiosity and adaptability rather than rigidity or fear of judgment. This sets the stage for them to develop a strong sense of self.

Redefining Social Connections as a Parent

Becoming a parent can redefine your social world in surprising ways, replacing spontaneous outings with bedtime routines and late-night talks with midnight feeds. Before having kids, I thrived on connection, spontaneous brunches, late-night conversations, and impromptu plans that added color to my life (fueled by my ADHD need to always get a dopamine hit). I never thought twice about a last-minute coffee date or staying out late with friends. Then, after our son was born, the invitations started to come less often. The friends who remained close were always thoughtful, but the logistics were different, and soon, I found myself unable to accept the invites I once jumped at. Sometimes, it was because of naptime or an unpredictable mood, other times simply because I was just exhausted. The changes crept up gradually but felt monumental.

I remember vividly the first time I turned down an invitation to a friend's dinner party. It felt strange, like I was choosing to step away from a part of myself, and a pang of sadness came with it, a small sense of loss. I wanted to keep those connections, but my world and schedule no longer matched up with the rhythm of my friends without kids. I found myself wondering, “Is this just temporary? Will I find my way back to that old version of me?” There were nights I scrolled through social media, seeing photos of friends out together, and felt a mix of longing and resentment, wanting to be there but also knowing I couldn’t show up in the same way anymore. The months passed, and I gradually started to find connection in new ways. Those stroller walks with other parents weren’t as spontaneous as brunches, but they offered something my former life couldn’t: a sense of shared understanding. I found myself leaning into quiet chats over tea while our little ones played nearby, laughing/crying about our messy mornings and unfinished conversations as our toddlers tugged at our sleeves. It wasn’t glamorous, but there was comfort in knowing I didn’t have to explain why I was late, distracted, or looked like I hadn’t washed my hair in days, because they were in the same place. There was a raw honesty in these connections that felt refreshing; these friends understood the highs and lows in ways I hadn’t needed from friendships before.

Although it was different from the social life I once knew, it was somehow more grounding. These new connections had a depth built on shared experience, on knowing that we’d all been awake at 2 a.m. with a feverish child or had moments of laughing while our toddlers painted the walls with yogurt. The conversations may be constantly interrupted, half-finished between diaper changes and snack requests, but they’re real, and they’re enough. My connections are fewer, yes, and the conversations often happen with a toy car rolling across my lap. But they are richer, founded on empathy and a mutual respect for the beauty and chaos that comes with raising kids. Parenthood redefined what friendship looks like, teaching me that connection isn’t just about the frequency of spontaneous meetups, but about the depth of shared experience. These friends are right beside me in the trenches, and that has made all the difference.

Resource: In *All Joy and No Fun,* Jennifer Senior explores the way parenting transforms friendships, capturing the challenges and rewarding connections that emerge during this stage.

PRE-CHILD PLANNING: **Anticipating Social Changes**

* How do you anticipate your social connections changing, and how does that make you feel?
* Are there friendships you expect to deepen as you become a parent, and why?
* What did your social world look like growing up? How did your caregivers approach connection, friendship, and community support?
* What assumptions do you hold about how much extended family or community should be involved in raising children? Where do those assumptions come from?
* How can you begin communicating your upcoming changes in priorities to your social circle or your family members?

DURING PREGNANCY: **Preparing for Evolving Social Dynamics**

* Which friendships feel most nourishing as you prepare for parenthood?
* How can you start exploring new ways to connect with friends, such as slower paced activities or virtual catch-ups?
* What feelings arise when you think about friendships that may fade, and how can you hold space for those emotions?

* Are there family members or community members you expect will want to be more involved, and how do you want to navigate that?

POSTPARTUM: **Nurturing Connection in the First Year**

* How have your social connections changed since becoming a parent, and how do those shifts make you feel?
* Which friendships feel most nourishing amid the demands of early parenting?
* In what ways have you found a deeper connection with other parents who understand your experiences?
* What role can family or chosen family play in supporting your social and emotional needs during this time?
* How do you set boundaries with well-meaning visitors who may not understand your current capacity?
* What do you miss about your pre-parent life, and how can you give yourself permission to talk about this without shame?

TODDLER YEARS: **Balancing Social and Family Life**

* What are the social commitments that bring you energy and joy, and how do you prioritize them?
* How do you balance your toddler's needs with your own need for connection?
* What new ways have you discovered to nurture your friendships, even with little ones in tow?
* Are there boundaries you need to communicate to relatives or caregivers around caregiving, hosting, or shared time?

4–8 YEARS: **Broadening Your Social Circle**

* How have school or activity-based connections shaped your social world?
* Which friendships feel harder to maintain as your child's schedule becomes busier?
* How do you prioritize the social commitments that align with your family's evolving lifestyle?
* How do you navigate expectations from extended family around holidays, birthdays, and social rituals?

9–12 YEARS: **Fostering Social Independence**

* How do you model healthy friendships for your preteen?
* What activities feel most meaningful to you as a parent to build or maintain connections?
* How can you balance supporting your preteen's social growth with nurturing your own social needs?
* What role do community or intergenerational relationships (like with grandparents, neighbors, mentors) play in your family's social life?

TEENAGERS: **Navigating Changing Social Priorities**

* How do you model healthy boundaries and relationships in your social connections for your teenager?
* How can you build shared social experiences with your teen, such as family events or cultural activities?
* What feelings arise when you reflect on your evolving social priorities, and how do you embrace those changes?

- How do you support your teen's relationships with extended family, and how do you model those yourself?

ADULT CHILDREN: **Redefining Relationships with Grown Children**

- How do you maintain meaningful connections with your adult children while fostering their independence?
- How do your friendships reflect the values and priorities you've cultivated over your parenting journey?
- What new relationships or activities have brought you joy in this stage of life?
- How do you continue to build or rebuild relationships with siblings, cousins, or the community as your parenting role shifts?

Navigating Family Expectations and Cultural Pressures

Family can be a source of comfort and connection, and it can also bring its own set of expectations, shaped by generations of traditions and well-meaning advice. Coming from Slovakia, I've always held my upbringing close to heart. In Slovak households, it's typical for children to share a room with their parents well into toddlerhood, and sleep training is virtually unheard of. Babies are comforted in close quarters, often soothed by being physically near their parents or with tools like soothers that are seen as essential for self-calming.

When my ex-husband and I decided to sleep train our son at six months and later our daughter at five months, it felt like a bold departure from these traditional ways, and I knew my mother would have strong feelings about it. She tried to be gentle but was clearly concerned. She wondered aloud if it was best for the baby and suggested we rearrange our bedroom to fit the crib, just as she and my dad had done for my sister and me. When we mentioned we'd be removing the soother too, she was baffled. I could sense that her advice came from deep care, but also from a worldview that didn't match the one we were parenting in. And beneath her words, I could hear the unspoken: "This isn't how it's done in our family." That cut deep, because even though I believed in our choice, I also carried the guilt of feeling like I was rejecting a piece of my culture and her wisdom.

We believed sleep training might help all of us get more rest and support our mental health. The truth is, I was at the end of my rope. The constant wakings were taking a toll not just on my body but on my marriage. I found myself snapping with irritation in the middle of the night, crying in the bathroom, feeling like I was failing because I couldn't keep functioning on so little sleep. But the first several nights weren't easy. Listening to our baby cry, even for a few minutes, went against every fiber of my upbringing. I paced the hallway with tears in my own eyes, wondering if I was making a mistake. But slowly, with consistency, the wakings lessened, and we all started to breathe again. The relief of an unbroken stretch of sleep reminded me that supporting my kids also meant supporting myself. To her credit, my mother watched patiently and eventually saw the benefits. She understood that our choices, while different from hers, came from love, too. I'll never forget the night she quietly admitted, "He really does sleep better now." It felt like a bridge between us, her way of saying she saw me, even if she wouldn't have chosen the same path. That moment helped me realize that honoring family traditions doesn't always mean doing things the same way. Sometimes, it means holding the values behind them—comfort, connection, and care—while letting go of the methods. Parenting means learning to walk that line between honoring where we come from and building something new.

Resource: Books like *The Awakened Family* by Dr. Shefali Tsabary offer perspective on how to hold space for tradition while making room for individual values and needs.

PRE-CHILD PLANNING: **Exploring Your Cultural and Family Values**

* What messages did you receive growing up about what a "good" parent should be?
* How did your family express love, discipline, and responsibility, and how do you feel about those models now?
* Which cultural or family traditions feel important to carry forward, and which might you want to rework or leave behind?
* How do you imagine extended family members responding to your parenting style or boundaries?
* What role would you like grandparents, relatives, or your community to play in raising your child?
* How will your upbringing shape how you involve (or set limits with) your "village"?

DURING PREGNANCY: **Preparing for Family Input**

* What kinds of advice or opinions have you already received from extended family, and how are you responding?
* How do you plan to communicate your parenting choices when they differ from family traditions?
* What feelings come up when you imagine being questioned or judged by relatives?

* What would it look like to involve extended family in ways that feel helpful, not overwhelming?
* Are there clear boundaries you want to set before the baby arrives?

POSTPARTUM: **Navigating Family Expectations and Traditions**

* What aspects of your cultural background or family expectations have shown up in the early postpartum period?
* How do your current parenting choices align with, or challenge, your family's traditions or values?
* In what ways do you find yourself trying to please others when making decisions for your baby?
* How do you respond when someone close to you questions or contradicts your parenting choices?
* Are there ways to include extended family meaningfully while still honoring your boundaries and needs?
* What traditions (feeding, soothing, sleep, etc.) are being passed down, and how do you feel about continuing or adapting them?

TODDLER YEARS: **Navigating Expectations Around Discipline and Routines**

* How does your approach to discipline differ from the way you were raised, and how do you explain this to family members?
* What expectations do extended family members hold around mealtimes, behavior, or routines, and how do they align with yours?

- How do you handle criticism or commentary from relatives during family gatherings or holidays?
- How do you help your toddler feel connected to cultural or family traditions without reinforcing patterns you disagree with?
- What's your comfort level with saying no to family requests or input that conflict with your values?

4–8 YEARS: **Expanding Cultural Awareness**

- How do you talk to your child about their cultural background in ways that feel authentic to your current family structure?
- Which family traditions have you kept, changed, or created, and how have those decisions been received?
- How do you handle it when your child prefers modern or different customs from what your family expects?
- Are there relatives who try to "teach" or pass on certain values to your child? Do you agree with those messages?
- How do you support your child's curiosity while setting limits on cultural or religious expectations from others?

9–12 YEARS: **Fostering Independence While Honoring Traditions**

- How do you talk to your child about your cultural values in a way that honors both their independence and your roots?
- What traditions feel essential to maintain, and what are you open to evolving?

* How do you navigate when your preteen questions a family custom or ritual?
* What expectations might extended family still hold about your child's behavior or participation in cultural practices?
* How do you support your child in respectfully pushing back or setting boundaries with relatives?

TEENAGERS: **Balancing Cultural Roots with Emerging Identities**

* What is your teen rejecting or questioning about your family's traditions, and how do you respond?
* How do you stay connected to your roots while giving your teen room to develop their own beliefs and identity?
* What messages do you want your teen to hear from extended family, and which ones do you need to buffer or reframe?
* How do you talk with your teen about the difference between honoring traditions and blindly following them?
* How can family rituals evolve to include your teen's voice and needs?

ADULT CHILDREN: **Evolving Family Traditions**

* How do you manage expectations around traditions, holidays, or rituals with your adult child and their evolving family life?
* What has shifted in your role? Are you still trying to pass on certain values or traditions? How is that received?

- How do you show respect for your adult child's autonomy while still expressing your hopes for family or cultural continuity?
- What stories, recipes, or values do you want to pass down, and what are you willing to let go of?
- How do you see your extended family's involvement with future generations (e.g., grandparenting, shared caregiving)?

People-Pleasing in Parenting

People-pleasing often sneaks into parenting in ways we don't expect. Between managing family opinions, meeting our children's needs, and keeping up with friends, the tendency to say yes can feel almost automatic. I've always leaned into being "kind," doing what I can to make others comfortable, feeling responsible for others' happiness. But over time, I realized that some of my "kindness" wasn't rooted in authentic care; it was actually a pattern of people-pleasing, a "fawn" response that I had developed as a way to avoid conflict or disappointment. People-pleasing in this way can feel like kindness, but deep down, it's often about managing fear or discomfort rather than genuine empathy. When I became a parent, this urge to please only intensified. I was doing everything I could to meet everyone's expectations, taking on more than my share of housework so my ex wouldn't feel stressed, agreeing to visits with extended family even when I was bone-tired, and following advice I didn't actually believe in just to avoid judgment. And of course, I was trying to live up to a variety of opinions on how to raise my children. Everywhere I turned, it felt like someone had a strong opinion: feed this way, parent that way, don't coddle, don't be too strict. And instead of tuning into myself, I bent in whatever direction felt safest in the moment.

There was a weekend that stands out in my mind, a string of social events and plans where I'd said yes to everything. Friday evening, we were out to dinner, Saturday was filled with a trip to the farmers' market with friends, and Sunday, we spent at a family gathering. By Sunday night, every member of my household, down to the newborn, was exhausted, each of us stretched thin and irritable. I felt depleted, and, in hindsight, I realized I'd agreed to everything that weekend not out of true enthusiasm, but because I couldn't bear the thought of letting anyone down. I even remember nursing my baby in the corner at that family gathering, aching to go home, while nodding and smiling at conversations I wasn't really present for. My body was screaming for rest, but my mouth kept saying "Of course, yes, we'll stay a little longer." That weekend helped me see how much my people-pleasing habits were impacting my family. At that moment, I understood that I needed to make a shift both for myself and for my family's well-being. Learning to set boundaries as a parent has been one of the hardest, yet most necessary, lessons. I'm working to understand that kindness doesn't mean saying yes to everyone. Sometimes, the most loving thing we can do is to say no, to preserve the calm and connection in our family. That means texting friends "We can't make it this time" without overexplaining, or telling my mom, "We're skipping this weekend, we just need rest," even when I know she'll sound disappointed. And then holding steady in that discomfort, reminding myself that the short-term guilt is worth the long-term peace.

Understanding the distinction between what I think I need to do to make other people like me versus what would actually be most helpful for me to take care of myself and my family has been empowering. Now, through self-reflection (and my own therapy), I have learned that true kindness doesn't require self-sacrifice; it's about honoring our own needs alongside those of others. Setting boundaries is a way to offer the best version of ourselves, and I'm working each day to embrace the idea that saying no doesn't mean I'm letting anyone down. Instead, it's a sign of respect for my family's needs, my own well-being, and, ultimately, the relationships that mean the most to me.

Resource: *Adult Children of Emotionally Immature Parents* by Lindsay C. Gibson sheds light on how early patterns of people-pleasing develop, offering strategies for reclaiming boundaries.

PRE-CHILD PLANNING: **Recognizing People-Pleasing Tendencies Before Parenthood**

- How did people-pleasing show up in your family growing up? Were you rewarded for being agreeable, compliant, or helpful?
- What messages did you internalize about conflict, saying no, or prioritizing your own needs?
- In what ways do you fear disappointing others when it comes to future parenting decisions?
- How might the urge to please others shape how you plan to parent, especially in front of extended family, friends, or your community?
- What would it look like to parent from your values, even if that means disappointing someone?

DURING PREGNANCY: **Setting the Foundation for Healthy Boundaries**

- What emotions arise when family or friends give unsolicited advice about your pregnancy or upcoming parenting choices?
- How do you imagine handling moments when others expect you to follow certain cultural or family norms?

* What is your relationship to saying no or not right now?
* How will you handle offers for help or involvement that don't feel aligned with your needs?
* How can you stay connected to loved ones while also practicing early boundary-setting?

POSTPARTUM: **Setting Boundaries While Staying Connected**

* What pressures, spoken or unspoken, are you noticing from others about how to be a "good" parent?
* When have you said yes to something out of guilt or obligation, and how did it affect your well-being?
* How do you manage feelings of guilt when prioritizing your needs or your baby's needs over others' expectations?
* What stories do you tell yourself when you say no, and where do those stories come from?
* Who in your extended family, friend group, or community struggles to respect your boundaries, and how are you navigating that?
* What kinds of support help you feel more confident in honoring your instincts, and which ones tend to reinforce people-pleasing?

TODDLER YEARS: **Teaching Boundaries by Modeling Them**

* What does it bring up in you when your toddler pushes back or says no, and how might that mirror your discomfort with assertiveness?
* When others offer treats, toys, or parenting tips that contradict your values, how do you respond?

✱ How do you talk about boundaries with your toddler, and how do you show them that it's okay to disappoint others?
✱ Are there certain people or settings where you find it harder to hold your ground?
✱ What do you notice about your people-pleasing patterns when your child is upset in public or in front of others?

4–8 YEARS: **Fostering Agency and Resilience in Children**

✱ How do you model boundary-setting in your daily life, especially when it comes to social obligations or extended family pressure?
✱ When your child expresses frustration or disappointment, how do you manage your urge to "fix it" or avoid discomfort?
✱ How can you support your child's autonomy without sacrificing your comfort or capacity?
✱ Are there social circles or community spaces where you feel pressure to present a version of yourself that isn't sustainable?
✱ What are you teaching your child, directly or indirectly, about their responsibility for other people's emotions?

9–12 YEARS: **Encouraging Independence While Maintaining Connection**

✱ How do you support your child's increasing independence without over-accommodating or overcorrecting?
✱ What role does guilt play in your parenting at this stage, and how do you work with it?
✱ How do you model standing up for yourself with extended family, friends, or community?

* When your child expresses needs that conflict with your plans or preferences, how do you respond?
* What boundaries are you practicing now that would have felt too hard a few years ago?

TEENAGERS: **Helping Teens Recognize and Resist People-Pleasing**

* How do you talk to your teen about peer pressure, emotional caretaking, or the need to please?
* What have you learned about your people-pleasing tendencies that you want to share with your teen?
* How do you model saying no without apology, and what messages does your teen pick up from that?
* When your teen pushes back, how do you balance your desire to be liked with your responsibility to parent?
* Are there patterns of conflict-avoidance or over-accommodation that you notice repeating from your upbringing?

ADULT CHILDREN: **Evolving Boundaries in Adult Relationships**

* How do you navigate your role as a parent when your adult child makes choices you disagree with?
* What people-pleasing habits show up in your adult relationships, with your child, in-laws, or community?
* How do you stay connected without feeling responsible for your adult child's emotions or outcomes?

* When you feel compelled to give advice, do you check in with yourself about why?
* What would it mean to trust your adult child to set their own boundaries, even if that means setting some with you?

Chapter 2

PARENTING IN THE DIGITAL AGE

Our children are growing up in a world where screens are as common as books, and digital experiences are woven into everyday life. Parenting in the digital age includes navigating screen time, social media, online interactions, and the shifting landscape of digital influence. It requires us to teach our kids to use technology mindfully, helping them develop self-regulation and digital literacy, and fostering their self-worth in an online-centric world. This chapter is about finding a balanced approach to technology that supports your family's well-being, creating boundaries that feel sustainable, and encouraging mindful habits that reflect your values.

The Psychology of Screen Time and Digital Influence

From a psychological perspective, digital devices have a profound impact on both children and adults. Research shows that screens activate the brain's reward system by releasing dopamine, a "feel-good" chemical that makes screen interactions engaging, and, at times, hard to step away from. For children, excessive screen time can overstimulate, leading to post-screen irritability, difficulty transitioning, and disrupted sleep patterns. For parents, screens can offer much-needed relief during challenging moments, but reliance on them can sometimes lead to feelings of guilt or disconnection.

Social media adds another layer of complexity, introducing the concept of social comparison, where children and adults alike evaluate themselves against the curated lives they see online. For young minds, this can create unrealistic expectations of appearance, success, or happiness, potentially impacting self-esteem. Teaching children to approach digital spaces with critical thinking and resilience helps them navigate these pressures with confidence and self-awareness.

Why Mindful Digital Habits Matter

Mindful use of technology teaches children to see screens as tools rather than defaults, encouraging them to balance their digital and offline lives. When parents set intentional boundaries and model healthy screen habits, they help children develop emotional regulation, build real-world confidence, and approach the digital world with awareness. By fostering open communication about technology, parents can also create a sense of safety and trust, empowering children to make thoughtful choices as they grow.

In this chapter, we'll explore strategies for setting screen time boundaries, teaching digital literacy, and promoting self-worth in a hyperconnected world. Together, we'll uncover how to balance technology's benefits with its challenges, creating a family environment that prioritizes connection, self-awareness, and mutual respect.

Setting Healthy Screen Time Boundaries

Finding the right balance with screen time has been one of the more difficult parenting challenges for me, especially on the days when it feels like the only thing that can buy me a moment to breathe. One rainy weekend really sticks with me. We'd already cycled through every activity I could think of: crafts, books, smoothie-making, and a pretend picnic in the living room. By early afternoon, we were all getting restless. I finally put on my son's favorite show (shout-out to *Blippi*). For a while, it brought that sweet, quiet pause we were all craving. I checked a few messages, caught my breath, and felt like I could finally sit down.

But when it came time to turn it off, everything shifted. My son was upset, more irritable than before, and his whole mood felt off. He whined, resisted, and eventually stormed off. I felt that familiar wave of guilt roll in. I had leaned on the screen to get through a tough moment, but now it felt like it had backfired. I caught myself thinking, "Why did I do that? I should've held out a little longer." But the truth was, I was running on fumes, and that pause kept me from completely losing it. That night, while replaying the day, I caught myself spiraling into shame, but then I paused. The reality is, I'd used the screen to get a real need met: rest. I needed a break. And the truth is, in today's world, parents are often carrying a lot without much support. Him melting down afterward didn't mean I had failed; it just meant we needed to regulate together again. That's part of the push and pull of parenting—sometimes we get it right, sometimes we muddle through.

My kids' dad works in film, so his schedule isn't your typical nine-to-five. He often has to check his phone for last-minute auditions, on-set calls, or client emails. There have definitely been times when his screen time has felt like it pulls him away from being present with our children, something we've talked about many times in the past and tried to set rules and boundaries with. We've had to get honest for our kids and ourselves, too. With ADHD in the mix for both my ex-husband and me (both of us late diagnosed as adults after having kids), the pull of screens can be even stronger. It's not just about entertainment; sometimes it's the dopamine hit of scrolling, the quick escape from overstimulation, or the buffer when our brains feel maxed out. It's harder to shift attention, harder to stop once we've started, and harder still to stay fully present without a sensory buffer. We would try to stay away from our screens during mealtimes or intentional play time, and when we forgot to, my toddler would have no problem with saying, "Mama, can you put your phone down?"

I've also seen a wide range of approaches to screens in the families around us. Some friends let their kids use screens early on, while others have been much more structured or even strict about avoiding screens altogether. What stands out to me, though, is that these families, despite their very different approaches, are all raising kind, connected, and happy kids. That nuance is something I try to hold onto, especially when my feed is full of posts warning about the harms of any screen use. There's a lot of messaging out there that can make you feel like a bad parent if you rely on screens, even occasionally, but what those videos don't show is the reality of parenting without a village. Sometimes, screens are the only way we get to make dinner, shower, or just sit down for a period of time without someone needing us.

We've come to see screen time not as inherently bad, but as something that can be either helpful or harmful depending on how it's used. We try to reserve it for moments that feel intentional, and we've started building in other types of moments too, like solo play, music, or being silly on the couch together. Some days screens barely come on, and other days I'm turning on Ms. Rachel at 7 a.m. because survival feels more important than ideals. But when we use it thoughtfully, it feels less like a crutch and more like one of many tools we can reach for. We're doing our best to model balance, knowing that connection, attunement, and presence are what matter most, and that sometimes, the screen is the break that makes real connection possible again.

Resource: *Screenwise* by Devorah Heitner is an excellent resource for setting thoughtful screen boundaries with kids. It provides practical advice on balancing screen time, encouraging parents to consider quality over quantity and to model healthy screen habits themselves.

PRE-CHILD PLANNING: **Setting the Foundation for Screen Habits**

* What messages did each of you grow up with around screen time? Was it allowed freely, limited, or shamed?
* How do you currently use screens for rest, connection, or stimulation? Where do you notice it helps or hurts your well-being?
* What role might sensory needs or overstimulation play in your relationship to screens?
* How might your habits around phone use or TV shape the way you parent?
* Do you and your partner or co-parent have different patterns or needs when it comes to screen use? What conversations could help align your values?
* Who else might be part of your caregiving village, and how do you want to talk with them about screen boundaries?

DURING PREGNANCY: **Planning for Mindful Screen Use as a Family**

- What expectations or pressures are already surfacing about "doing it right" when it comes to screen time?
- What do you hope screen time will offer you as a new parent: comfort, breaks, background noise, shared moments?
- What fears or hesitations do you have about using screens during early parenthood?
- How can you and your partner or co-parent talk about screen boundaries ahead of time, especially when one or both of you might use devices for work or emotional regulation?
- Are there family members who may default to giving the baby a screen? How do you want to approach that conversation?

POSTPARTUM: **Reflecting on Screen Use Without Shame**

- In moments of exhaustion or sensory overload, how are you using screens, and how do you feel about it afterward?
- Are there routines like feeding, pumping, or contact naps where screen use feels comforting? Can you allow that without guilt?
- What does screen time look like in your household right now: structured, spontaneous, or background noise?
- Are you using screens to connect with others (like video calls with family), and how does that support or drain you?
- Are you holding shame or pressure to "do better" when it comes to screens? Where might that pressure be coming from?

* How are you and your partner/co-parent navigating each other's screen habits, especially if one person's phone use is tied to work?

TODDLER YEARS: **Introducing Boundaries and Alternatives**

* What kinds of screen-related meltdowns or negotiations are showing up, and what do they tell you about your toddler's regulation or routines?
* What screen-free activities help your toddler reset, and are they accessible on tough days?
* How do you explain screen limits to your child in a way that feels kind and consistent?
* In moments where screen time feels like the only option, what support do *you* wish you had instead?
* How do you and your partner divide the load when it comes to managing screen transitions?

4–8 YEARS: **Encouraging Play and Creativity Over Screens**

* What does your child enjoy most about screen time, and what might that say about what they're needing (e.g., quiet, learning, control)?
* How much input do you give your child in choosing screen content, and how do you guide that collaboratively?
* Are there screen rituals that have become part of your family culture, and do they still feel aligned with your values?
* How are you navigating requests for more screen time, especially on weekends, holidays, or after school?

- How do you talk with other parents or caregivers about different approaches to screen time without comparing or judging?

9–12 YEARS: **Teaching Self-Regulation Around Screens**

- Is your child starting to notice how screens impact their mood, attention, or energy?
- What conversations are you having about screen time as a tool for learning, connecting, or decompressing, rather than an escape?
- Is screen time ever a point of conflict in your home? How do you reconnect after?
- How can you and your child (and possibly partner) cocreate agreements about tech use that feel respectful and flexible?

TEENAGERS: **Fostering Mindful Tech Use and Independence**

- How do you stay connected to your teen's digital world? What are they watching? Who are they talking to? How do they unwind online?
- How do you talk about things like algorithmic content, doomscrolling, or tech and sleep hygiene?
- What screen rules or agreements still make sense in your home, and which ones need updating now that your child is older?
- In what ways do you model screen habits you feel good about, and where do you find it hard?
- What has your teen taught you about how they use technology, and are you open to learning from them?

ADULT CHILDREN: **Evolving Screen Habits and Family Dynamics**

* What screen habits do you see in your grown children that reflect what you modeled, and where have they created their own path?
* How do you stay connected with your adult child? Is it mostly texting, video calls, or in-person time? Are there ways to deepen connection across formats?
* During family time or holidays, how do you set boundaries or invitations for screen-free connection without forcing it?
* How do you navigate intergenerational screen differences when spending time with adult children and grandkids?
* What role do you want screens to play (or not play) in your relationship now?

Nurturing Digital Literacy and Ethics

In a world where so much of life happens online, teaching our kids about privacy and digital responsibility feels both daunting and necessary. I remember one summer afternoon, snapping a quick photo of my son splashing joyfully in his little pool in the backyard. The sunlight was perfect, capturing his smile, the dimples above his little bum, and the droplets flying around him. Without a second thought, I posted it to social media, eager to share the happy moment. But later that evening, as I scrolled through my feed and saw his photo among countless others, I felt a sudden wave of unease. A question lingered in my mind: *Who is seeing this?* I realized I hadn't given much thought to who would view that photo, or if sharing it was necessary at all. There was something unsettling about how easily that private moment had become part of the public space, a space that's hard to control once we release an image into it. It struck me that once something is online, it's no longer just ours. It felt like a punch to the gut: I had put him out there without thinking twice, and suddenly I couldn't take it back. The responsibility of protecting our little ones from online predators can feel overwhelming, especially when you realize that simply posting a photo with small emojis covering private areas isn't enough to keep them safe from those who might want to cause harm. Even the thought of strangers seeing his picture through a lens I hadn't intended made my stomach turn.

That small experience opened up a deeper conversation within our family about online privacy and respecting our children's digital boundaries. His dad and I began talking about how much we want to protect not only our kids' digital footprint but also their right to control their own story as they grow.

Over time, these conversations have evolved into family values around digital respect. We discuss how much thought to give before posting, ensuring that the content aligns with what we'd want our kids to look back on one day. Sometimes that means choosing not to post at all, or sending a funny photo to grandparents privately instead of uploading it to Instagram. And sometimes it means catching myself mid-scroll, realizing I'm about to share something out of habit rather than intention. We hope to teach our kids that privacy is something to be actively protected. When they're a little older and start using technology more independently, they'll have seen our efforts and values around intentionality and consent. In our digital age, these conversations are foundational. We're far from perfect; I still have moments where I post and second-guess myself later, but we're trying to model what it looks like to pause, to ask questions, and to change course if needed. And by fostering this awareness, we hope to guide them toward a responsible, mindful approach to the online world, encouraging them to consider the weight of each post, photo, and moment they choose to share.

Resource: *Raising Humans in a Digital World* by Diana Graber offers a comprehensive guide to teaching children about digital literacy, privacy, and respectful online behavior. It's filled with tools to help kids navigate online spaces thoughtfully and responsibly.

These conversation starters will help you explore your family's beliefs and practices around technology, privacy, and online sharing as your child grows.

PRE-CHILD PLANNING: **Establishing Family Values Around Digital Privacy**

* How do you currently manage your digital privacy, and how might that change with a child in the picture?
* What values around privacy and autonomy did you grow up with, and how have those influenced your online habits?
* When sharing updates or pictures of your future child, who do you want to have access to them?
* What boundaries around online sharing feel right for your family values?

DURING PREGNANCY: **Starting Conversations About Digital Boundaries**

* What are your thoughts about sharing ultrasound photos, bump updates, or baby news online?
* How do you want to handle well-meaning family members who might post about your child without asking?

* How do you feel about the idea of a digital footprint, and what steps can you take to protect your child's privacy?

POSTPARTUM: **Sharing Your Baby's Image Thoughtfully**

* Who can see the updates or photos you share of your child, and are you comfortable with that audience?
* How do you navigate situations where others post photos of your baby online without asking?
* What do you want to model for your child about consent and online sharing, even at this early stage?
* How do you talk to family or friends about asking permission before posting photos of your baby?
* What might the digital content you share now mean for your child's future sense of privacy and autonomy?
* Are there systems you can set up (like password protection or shared agreements) to support your family's digital boundaries?

TODDLER YEARS: **Introducing Early Lessons About Privacy and Technology**

* How do you model healthy tech habits during routines like meals, playtime, or bedtime?
* How can you begin to introduce the idea of asking permission to take or share photos?
* What simple language can you use to help toddlers begin understanding personal boundaries?

4–8 YEARS: **Teaching the Basics of Digital Literacy**

* How can you explain a digital footprint in ways that make sense for your child's age and curiosity?
* How do you prepare your child for potential online risks without creating fear?
* What are some age-appropriate online tools or games that teach digital consciousness and safety?

9–12 YEARS: **Fostering Critical Thinking and Online Ethics**

* How can you help your preteen think critically about what they post or engage with online?
* How do you support them in navigating online friendships or potential negativity on the internet?
* What conversations can help them recognize the importance of kindness and consent in digital spaces?

TEENAGERS: **Encouraging Responsible and Ethical Online Behavior**

* How do you support your teen in balancing online life with offline relationships?
* How do you talk with them about long-term digital consequences, like their online reputation?
* What can you do to stay involved in their online world without being overly intrusive?

ADULT CHILDREN: **Modeling Lifelong Digital Literacy and Respect**

* How do you navigate sharing family photos or stories now that your children are adults?

- What values about digital ethics and boundaries do you hope your children carry with them?
- How can you respectfully collaborate on how your family appears online, especially across generations?

Social Media and Its Impact on Self-Image

Social media has this unique way of drawing us in with connection and inspiration, but it can just as easily stir up feelings of comparison and self-doubt. I'll never forget an afternoon when I was scrolling through my feed while my son napped peacefully beside me. Post after post flashed by, moments that looked polished and perfect: moms effortlessly balancing a toddler on one hip and a beautiful layered latte in the other hand, somehow glowing after a workout, going on fancy dates with their partners looking perfect, or standing proudly in kitchens filled with freshly baked cookies, bread, and homemade crafts. Each image felt meticulously curated, and even though I knew that, I couldn't shake the tug of inadequacy it stirred in me. I found myself wondering, *Am I doing enough for my kids? Am I present enough, creative enough, or "together" enough? Does my husband still find me attractive?* And in the background of all those questions was the quiet but relentless comparison soundtrack: "She's doing better than me. I should be more like that. Why can't I get it together?" It amazed me how quickly just a few images could make me question myself, the choices I was making, and my sense of worth as a parent (and partner). Rationally, I knew these images represented only tiny snapshots of reality, yet the self-doubt lingered. The polished glimpses into others' lives started to feel like an unspoken measuring stick, and I began to worry if I was falling short of this idealized version of motherhood. I even caught myself pulling up my camera roll, scrolling through photos of my kids, wondering which ones would make my life "look" better if I posted them. That was the moment I realized just how deep the pull of comparison can run.

In that moment, a sobering thought crossed my mind: *If I feel this pressure now, what will it be like for my children someday?* When they inevitably enter these digital spaces, will they feel the same pressure to measure up, to curate, to be "enough" online? The thought was both grounding and eye-opening, reminding me that as much as I struggle with self-doubt from these feeds, my children will be stepping into this world at an even younger, more impressionable age.

This realization fueled my determination to nurture a self-worth in them that goes deeper than any "like" or filtered photo. I want them to know their value is inherent, not something to be validated or diminished by online approval. For me, it's less about perfect rules around screen time and more about building a strong inner compass. I want them to know who they are even when the internet tells them who they "should" be. Now, as I think about how to guide them, I try to take more intentional steps myself, to be mindful about what I consume and how I react to it. That means noticing when I'm spiraling, putting my phone down, and sometimes even saying out loud, "Wow, that post just made me feel not good enough," so my kids hear me naming it instead of silently absorbing it. I remind myself that behind every polished photo is a real person, probably with their own doubts and insecurities, just like me. By working to break the cycle of comparison within myself, I hope to help my children grow up in a home where they're encouraged to see themselves as enough, no matter what they encounter on a screen. For my children, I will focus on recognizing their effort, courage, vulnerability, and strength, offering compliments that honor who they are and what they've overcome, rather than limiting my praise to their appearance. And maybe, if they watch me wrestle honestly with my own comparisons, they'll learn that feeling "less than" is human, but it doesn't have to define their worth.

Resource: *iGen* by Dr. Jean M. Twenge explores the impact of social media on self-image and provides insights into how young people experience online pressure. It's a helpful resource for parents looking to support their children's self-worth and encourage offline confidence.

PRE-CHILD PLANNING: **Reflecting on Your Relationship with Social Media**

* How does social media impact your self-image or confidence, and how do you manage those feelings?
* What boundaries or habits around social media would you like to cultivate before introducing a child into the mix?
* How do you balance the positives of social media, like connection and inspiration, with the challenges of comparison?
* How do you want your future child to see you engage with your phone or social media: present, distracted, balanced?
* What examples from your upbringing around appearance, achievement, or comparison might be showing up when you scroll online now?

DURING PREGNANCY: **Preparing to Navigate Social Media as a Parent**

* How do you feel about sharing pregnancy updates or photos online, and who do you want to share them with?

- How does seeing other parents' or pregnancy journeys online impact your confidence or choices?
- How can you start modeling a healthy relationship with social media during this phase?
- Are there expectations or pressures you feel about looking a certain way during pregnancy that are tied to social media exposure?
- How can you involve your partner or extended family in conversations about what should or shouldn't be shared online?

POSTPARTUM: **Reflecting on Social Media and Early Parenthood**

- Have you noticed moments when you compare your parenting or family to what you see online, and how does that affect you?
- How does your social media use during downtime, such as nighttime feeds or contact naps, impact your mood or energy?
- What kinds of boundaries (time limits, unfollows, screen-free rituals) help protect your mental well-being?
- How do you decide which parenting moments to share publicly and which to keep private?
- What messages, spoken or unspoken, are you modeling for your child about how we document and present our lives?
- How can you stay grounded in your own instincts, especially when social media makes you second-guess yourself?

TODDLER YEARS: **Balancing Your Online Presence with Offline Connection**

* How does sharing updates about your toddler online reflect your family's values?
* What routines can help you balance the benefits of social media with time for real-life connection?
* How do you notice your toddler reacting to your phone or screen time? Do they seek attention or try to engage with the screen?
* What kind of presence do you want to model for them when they're looking for your attention?

4–8 YEARS: **Introducing Concepts of Self-Worth Beyond Social Media**

* How can you talk to your child about the difference between online personas and real-life identity?
* What language can you use to explain the concept of "likes" and why they don't define value?
* How can you model confidence in your choices, even when social media suggests a "perfect" way to parent?
* How do you support your child in feeling proud of themself in everyday life, not just when others are watching?
* How can you involve extended family in reinforcing your child's intrinsic strengths and efforts over appearance or achievements?

9–12 YEARS: **Helping Preteens Navigate Social Media Thoughtfully**

* How can you help your child notice how social media makes them feel, whether positive or negative?

* What would help your preteen take control of their online experience, like unfollowing accounts that don't uplift them?
* How can you encourage them to prioritize real-life connections and activities over online validation?
* How do you want your child to handle moments when they're excluded online or receive negative comments?
* How can you build their confidence in making digital choices that reflect who they are, not who they think they should be?

TEENAGERS: **Encouraging Ethical and Confident Social Media Use**

* How does your teenager feel about "likes" or comments on their posts, and how do you discuss their significance?
* How can you help your teen navigate the pressure to present a perfect version of themselves online?
* What language helps you talk about the reality behind "perfect" online lives?
* How do you support them when they encounter digital peer pressure or unrealistic beauty and success standards?
* How can you encourage digital creativity or expression that reflects their personality and interests?

ADULT CHILDREN: **Supporting Digital Confidence in Adulthood**

* What kinds of photos do you share of your adult children online, and have they consented to it?

* How can you continue to model a healthy relationship with social media in your own life?
* How do you encourage your adult child to maintain offline connections that support their well-being?
* What boundaries might you still want to uphold in sharing family moments online now that your child is grown?
* Do you find yourself posting photos of all your children evenly, or do you focus on certain kids or events more than others?

Chapter 3

FINANCIAL LITERACY IN PARENTING

Money is one of those topics that can feel deeply personal, and, for many of us, more than a little uncomfortable. When we become parents, financial literacy evolves into more than a skill; it becomes part of the foundation we build for our family. It includes things like managing expenses and saving for the future, as well as modeling values and teaching children the confidence to make thoughtful financial decisions as they grow.

The Psychology of Money and Family Dynamics

Psychologically, one of the biggest factors that influences our relationship with money is our early childhood experiences. Studies have shown that the way families discuss and handle money directly influences children's beliefs about financial security, spending, and saving. For some, money may symbolize stability and success; for others, it may trigger stress or fear. These early patterns often carry forward into adulthood, sometimes unconsciously, shaping how we approach finances in our own families.

When parents model healthy financial habits, like calmly discussing expenses instead of arguing, avoiding shame around how family members spend money, and having open conversations about budgeting, realistic spending, and intentional saving, they set the tone for how their children will view money. Kids who grow up seeing money handled with respect and clarity are more likely to develop positive financial habits themselves. By creating a home environment where money is talked about openly and without judgment, parents teach their children that money is simply a tool, not a source of fear or conflict. This foundation helps kids approach financial challenges with confidence, resilience, and a sense of empowerment.

Why Financial Literacy Matters

Teaching financial literacy means instilling values like patience, responsibility, and generosity. It empowers parents to align their spending with their family's priorities and goals, creating a sense of control and purpose. For children, financial literacy provides the tools to make informed decisions, whether it's saving for a new toy, budgeting an allowance, or planning for their future.

In this chapter, we'll explore how financial habits are shaped by upbringing, strategies for aligning family finances with shared goals, and ways to introduce economic concepts to children at every stage of development. My hope is that by the end, you'll feel empowered to approach money with confidence, purpose, and a sense of collaboration within your family.

Understanding Your Financial Inheritance

Our relationship with money is often shaped long before we have our own bank accounts. It begins in childhood, woven into our understanding of safety, stress, and what it means to feel "secure." For many of us, especially those raised in immigrant families or by parents who experienced hardship, our financial patterns are also about survival, protection, and the deep desire to give the next generation something more.

Growing up, my family carried the weight of starting over. My parents moved to Canada with very limited resources and no financial safety net. My dad worked entry-level jobs and my mom spent several years at home to raise us before she started working as well. There was a period of time when my dad got sick and wasn't able to work at all. At times, we lived on one income, and while our basic needs were always met—home-cooked meals, clothes from secondhand stores, fruit on the table—there was an undercurrent of anxiety. We rarely ate out or indulged in extras. When money was discussed, it would often be in hostile ways, where shame and blame crept into our home. I could feel the tension in the air when unexpected bills came in or big expenses loomed. I still remember my dad at the kitchen table, calculator in hand, sighing loudly while my mom quietly cleared dishes, both of them avoiding eye contact. Even as a child, I knew something was wrong, even if I didn't understand the numbers. I witnessed quiet sacrifices, unspoken worry, arguments led by fear, and the way financial pressure seeped into everyday moments.

Looking back, I understand now that my parents weren't trying to instill fear or scarcity in me. They were doing their best with what they had, navigating a new country, new systems, and the burden of trying to protect us from instability. But as kids, we absorb the atmosphere in the room, and the atmosphere around money in our house was tense. And still, those early experiences stayed with me. As an adult, I've had to notice how easily I tense up around surprise expenses, or how I cling to the idea of financial "safety" as a way to self-soothe. Even now, an unexpected car repair or a bigger grocery bill can make my chest tighten in ways that feel disproportionate, but really, it's my nervous system remembering old stress.

When my former partner and I were together, our financial habits sometimes clashed. For him, money was more neutral, even empowering, a means of freedom. For me, it carried emotional weight: fear, responsibility, and a drive to prevent hardship at all costs. It helped us to talk honestly about where those patterns came from, unpacking stories, family dynamics, and inherited beliefs. Some of our hardest conversations weren't actually about money itself but about what money *meant*; to me, stability and safety; to him, choice and possibility. Understanding this has helped me soften. I don't shame myself for the anxiety that used to show up when we would talk about money. I understand it now as a part of me that developed early on, when I learned that I needed to be careful and alert. And when I notice that part showing up, I try to meet it with compassion instead of judgment.

Naming the roots of financial fear can allow you to cocreate new habits, ones that honor both you and your partner's histories and hopes. You can learn to make space for security and joy, for saving and living. That can look like involving your kids in little choices, letting them help budget for a family outing or talking through why you're saving for something instead of buying it right away. You want them to feel money as a tool, not a threat, and to know that conversations about it don't have to end in silence or slammed doors.

Resource: *The Psychology of Money* by Morgan Housel. This book explores how emotions and past experiences shape our financial decisions, helping us understand that our habits around money often have roots in our early experiences. It's a valuable resource for parents wanting to look at their own financial patterns with self-compassion.

PRE-CHILD PLANNING: **Reflecting on Financial Habits Before Parenthood**

* What memories do both you and your partner/co-parent have around money growing up, and what emotions come up when you revisit them?
* What was modeled for you around financial risk, generosity, or saving?
* How did your caregivers' beliefs about money shape your sense of security or anxiety?
* What community or cultural influences shaped your family's approach to money?
* How might your upbringing affect the way you talk about or handle money with your future children?

DURING PREGNANCY: **Preparing for Financial Shifts as a Family**

* What financial habits or beliefs from your upbringing are you hoping to shift before your child arrives?
* How do emotional reactions to money (scarcity, fear, overspending) show up in this stage?
* Are there money narratives you'd like to rewrite together as a couple or as co-parents?
* How will you integrate support from extended family or community if finances are tight?

POSTPARTUM: **Understanding Your Money Story in Parenthood**

* When unexpected expenses arise, how do you emotionally respond, and where do those feelings come from?
* What early money messages from childhood or culture are you most aware of repeating, and how might you choose differently now?

- How do you and your partner talk about financial decisions, and what emotions or dynamics tend to show up in those conversations?
- In what ways are your financial choices influenced (or challenged) by your extended family's values or expectations?
- How can you show yourself compassion as you navigate inherited financial anxiety or scarcity patterns?
- What would it look like to begin healing your relationship with money as part of conscious, values-based parenting?

TODDLER YEARS: **Repeating or Rewriting Patterns**

- Are you repeating with your toddler the financial patterns you learned in your own upbringing? How so?
- How do your childhood experiences with money show up when setting limits with your toddler?
- How do comments from extended family (e.g., about toys, spending) influence your current financial decisions?
- What emotional stories do you carry about providing or saying no, and how do they shape your responses?

4–8 YEARS: **Reframing Scarcity and Abundance**

- How did your own experience of "wants" and "needs" growing up impact the way you respond to your child?
- How do your early lessons about fairness or scarcity show up when you set expectations or limits now?

* What feelings emerge when your child asks for things you didn't have growing up?
* How do you balance your financial values with those of community or school culture (e.g., birthday gifts, brand names)?

9–12 YEARS: **Exploring Financial Identity**

* How did your preteen years shape your beliefs about monetary independence?
* Are you unintentionally projecting financial fears or pressure onto your child based on your history?
* How do you navigate family traditions or holidays that involve money, and what do you hope to do differently?
* What role did your community or extended family play in shaping your money worldview, and how might this influence what you teach now?

TEENAGERS: **Breaking the Silence Around Money**

* What money-related dynamics or unspoken rules from your teenage years are you still carrying?
* How did your caregivers talk (or not talk) about things like credit, debt, or spending?
* How can you begin healing money shame or secrecy by being open with your teen?
* In what ways do you want to parent differently around money from how you were parented?

ADULT CHILDREN: **Rewriting the Legacy Together**

* How does your past influence your current expectations about supporting adult children financially?
* Are there inherited beliefs around independence or responsibility that need reevaluation?
* How do you want to evolve your relationship to giving, lending, or gifting within family systems?
* What stories about money legacy (inheritance, wealth, debt) are important to unpack with your adult child?

Aligning Financial Decisions with Shared Values and Goals

Money conversations are rarely just about numbers. They're shaped by what we value, what we've lived through, and what we hope to create. For many families, financial decisions are deeply personal, and deeply contextual. They reflect our histories, identities, and the kinds of support or barriers we've encountered along the way. What one family might call a "luxury" could be another family's lifeline. What feels like a smart investment to some might feel completely out of reach to others.

As someone with ADHD, I tend to live more day-to-day, and budgeting feels overwhelming and often unsustainable for me. I've downloaded every money app under the sun, set up beautiful spreadsheets, and then abandoned them after a week because it all felt too rigid. I'm great at making big plans but terrible at tracking the little details. My children's father, who also has ADHD, is more naturally strategic, and planning ahead helps him feel grounded. Over time, we've come to understand each other's nervous systems and needs more clearly, and we've started having deeper conversations about how we actually want to co-parent together. For us, one of our biggest shared values is time. Time with our kids, time to rest, time to not feel like we're running on fumes. That means we've made intentional choices to outsource certain tasks, like hiring cleaners once a month, using grocery delivery services, or subscribing to meal kits. These are decisions meant to protect our capacity and help us show up for the parts of life that matter most to us. It doesn't always feel comfortable, the guilt kicks in and I'll wonder if we "should" just do it all ourselves, but the reality is, outsourcing even small things has saved us from constant burnout. That said, we're aware that even having the option to make these decisions comes from a place of significant privilege.

We both have jobs, we have access to health care, live in a relatively stable communities, and have family support nearby. We're white, cisgender, and housed. Those layers of privilege shape the kinds of financial conversations we even get to have. Not every family has the option to hire support or say no to burnout. For many, financial decisions are about survival, not self-care or value alignment. I think about my parents, who didn't have the luxury of "outsourcing" anything. There were no cleaners, no meal kits, just long work hours and stretching every dollar. Remembering that keeps me humble. That perspective keeps us grounded when we talk about spending or goals. It reminds us to hold humility alongside choice. It's also why I don't believe there's a one-size-fits-all idea of "smart" money management. What works for one family can feel completely impossible for another. For some families, putting kids in daycare full-time is essential for paying rent. For others, staying home and saving on childcare is the only option. Some might prioritize education savings, while others prioritize extended family support or paying down generational debt. A single parent might need to outsource meals just to make it through the week.

A marginalized family might spend more on community-based programs to give their kids a sense of belonging. Someone with a chronic illness might invest in services or tools to maintain stability. There is no universal blueprint, and what feels like a "shared goal" will look different depending on your cultural background, access to resources, health status, immigration experience, disability, family structure, and more. So, when we talk about values, it's important to remember that those values don't exist in a vacuum. They're shaped by what we've had to carry and what we've had to overcome.

Resource: *Financial Feminist* by Tori Dunlap is a modern, values-based guide to money that explores how gender, systemic inequality, and internalized beliefs affect financial choices. It's accessible and grounded in real-life scenarios, making it ideal for parents who want to explore how their financial habits intersect with their identity and values.

PRE-CHILD PLANNING: **Identifying Financial Values as a Couple or as Co-Parents**

* What do you each believe makes a life "rich," and how do those beliefs influence your spending?
* How did your early experiences with money shape your sense of safety, fairness, or worth?
* Are there cultural, racial, or class-based expectations around money that still impact you today?
* In what ways do you approach financial decision-making differently, and how can you hold space for both perspectives?
* Which values do you hope will guide your money choices as you become parents?

DURING PREGNANCY: **Communicating About Financial Priorities**

* Which financial choices are helping you build the kind of life you want to live, right now and in the future?
* Are you feeling pressure to buy or plan things a certain way based on what others around you are doing?
* What does "responsible" spending look like to each of you, and where did those ideas come from?
* How can you check in gently when you feel misaligned, especially during a time of emotional and hormonal shifts?
* Are there privileges you have now that your families didn't have, and how do they impact your choices?

POSTPARTUM: **Exploring Shared Financial Values and Emotional Spending**

* What are you spending money on that genuinely helps you feel more connected, cared for, or less overwhelmed?
* Are you noticing different emotional reactions to saving, spending, or financial planning, and how can you make room for both?
* Do you feel like financial responsibilities are being shared fairly, even if not divided equally?
* How do you talk about outsourcing support (like meals, childcare, or cleaning) in a way that centers care rather than shame?
* How do extended family or cultural expectations shape what you feel you "should" be buying or doing financially?

- What does financial flexibility look like for you and your partner right now, and how can you practice compassion for yourselves in this season?

TODDLER YEARS: **Navigating Differing Approaches**

- When you disagree on spending (toys, programs, gear), how can you stay curious instead of reactive?
- Are there unspoken rules or roles you've taken on around money that need reworking?
- What feels like an intentional investment versus something you feel pressured into?
- How do you talk about money choices with others (e.g., in-laws, friends) who might not understand your values?
- What money decisions are helping you avoid burnout, and do you feel okay about them?

4–8 YEARS: **Teaching Through Daily Choices**

- How are you modeling mindful or values-based spending in everyday routines?
- What lessons are you passing on, intentionally or not, about money, time, and rest?
- Do your financial habits reflect what you say you care about, or are there areas you want to revisit?
- Are you spending money in ways that bring joy or connection, or just to keep up?
- How do you handle situations where your values differ from those of other families at school or in the community?

9–12 YEARS: **Building Financial Teamwork**

* How can you start bringing your child into conversations about money in age-appropriate ways?
* Are you aligned on what financial independence means at this age?
* What peer or cultural pressures are influencing your spending, and how do you want to respond?
* Are you teaching your child about money in a way that reflects both your realities and your hopes for their future?
* Where do your parenting goals clash with financial realities, and how can you support each other there?

TEENAGERS: **Preparing for Value-Based Independence**

* What money messages are you giving your teen, and how might they be interpreted based on your habits or tone?
* Are you including your teen in decisions about family spending where appropriate, or shielding too much?
* What fears or hopes do you have about their financial future, and how can you share them without projecting?
* How do you want to prepare them for life in a world where access, privilege, and equity vary widely?
* What mistakes or lessons about money from your teenage years do you want to talk about?

ADULT CHILDREN: **Collaborating Across Generations**

* How do you navigate differences in financial choices without judgment or comparison?
* Are you aligned on what financial support looks like from others, such as gifts, loans, inheritances, and time?
* What shared goals (e.g., supporting grandchildren, travel, elder care) are important to name and plan for?
* How do you keep conversations open and respectful as everyone's lives and priorities evolve?
* What legacy do you want to leave, financially, emotionally, or otherwise?

Teaching Financial Literacy to Your Children

Teaching kids about money doesn't have to come from a textbook or even a formal sit-down conversation. So much of what children learn about money comes from what they see, hear, and absorb in daily life: how we talk about spending, how we respond to financial stress, what we value in our choices, and how we model generosity, gratitude, or restraint. Even the silences or tensions around money teach something. That's why it's less about delivering the "right" financial lesson and more about staying aware of what messages we're giving through our habits and reactions.

With our kids still quite young, we're starting small. This year, for my son's fourth Christmas, I'm planning to get him a piggy bank, something simple, tactile, and playful. My goal is to introduce the idea that money has value and can be saved toward something meaningful.

It might start with tossing in spare change and chatting about what he wants to save for, like a small toy, an outing, or a sticker book. Honestly, I know he'll probably dump the coins out more than he'll save them, but that's part of it, making money feel concrete instead of abstract. These early moments aren't about rigid lessons; they're about building a foundation where money isn't mysterious or anxiety-inducing, but rather something he can understand and engage with over time.

Of course, what we're able to teach our children, and how we teach it, is shaped by our context. We know that introducing financial literacy is a privilege in itself. It assumes there's some level of stability, choice, and access. There are nights I remind myself that even having spare change for a piggy bank is a form of privilege, because not every family has that margin. Some families are navigating food insecurity or housing instability. Others are carrying debt from generational hardship, immigration, or systemic discrimination. For those families, "saving" may not be a priority, and it may not even be possible. And that's important to acknowledge when we talk about teaching money skills.

As our kids get older, we plan to build on this foundation, introducing ideas like needs versus wants, discussing how we make decisions around giving and spending, and involving them in small family choices when appropriate. That might look like letting them help choose what's for dinner when we're planning meals on a budget, or explaining why we're waiting to buy something instead of grabbing it right away. We also want to talk to them about fairness in a broader sense, specifically in terms of economic justice, like why some kids at school don't always bring lunch, why not everyone can afford field trips, or how our neighbors' experiences might look different from ours. We hope that teaching financial literacy will help our children understand the role money plays in their lives and the lives of others, and how values like equity, empathy, and responsibility can shape their choices in the future.

Resource: *The Opposite of Spoiled* by Ron Lieber is an excellent guide for parents who want to teach kids about money in a way that feels empowering, honest, and values-based. It's full of simple ways to introduce financial literacy, from allowance strategies to lessons on generosity.

PRE-CHILD PLANNING: **Envisioning Your Role as Financial Teacher**

* What kind of financial education did you receive (or not receive) growing up?
* What kind of relationship with money do you hope to model for your child?
* How comfortable do you feel teaching about money? Where might you need to learn more?
* How do you want to talk about privilege, hard work, or fairness in your family?

DURING PREGNANCY: **Planning for Age-Appropriate Lessons**

* What financial values or concepts do you and your partner want to begin introducing from the start?
* How can you build financial literacy into everyday family life, not just one-off talks?
* How do you plan to discuss topics like gifts, savings, or spending with extended family?
* Are there differences in your and your partner's beliefs about what kids "need to know" and when?

POSTPARTUM: **Laying the Groundwork**

* What financial language do you both want to normalize early (e.g., "budget," "saving," "value")?
* How are you making choices that reflect what you hope to teach, even before your child understands?
* Are you setting up long-term tools (529 plans, RESPs, savings) that reflect teaching through action?
* How do you balance modeling confidence with being honest about financial limits?

0–1 YEARS: **Modeling Through Tone and Behavior**

* How do you respond when talking about money in front of your baby (even if they don't understand yet)?
* What habits are you beginning to form that will one day teach your child what's "normal" around money?
* How do you react emotionally to financial decisions, and what might you be modeling nonverbally?

TODDLER YEARS: **Beginning Early Conversations**

* How do you introduce basic concepts like "cost," "saving," or "sharing" in toddler-friendly ways?
* What stories, books, or play opportunities can help build early money awareness?
* Are you consistent in explaining that you can't always buy everything, and why?
* How do you involve toddlers in small decisions that begin to build financial curiosity?

4–8 YEARS: **Building Financial Language and Routine**

* How do you explain the difference between "wants" and "needs" in day-to-day life?
* What simple money routines can you create together, like piggy banks or jars for saving/spending?
* How do you respond to peer pressure-related requests (e.g., toys, clothes) in a values-aligned way?
* How do you teach gratitude and generosity alongside financial understanding?

9–12 YEARS: **Introducing Responsibility**

* Are you giving them opportunities to earn, save, or spend their own money with guidance?
* What financial tasks (e.g., budgeting for a birthday, grocery list planning) can you involve them in?
* How do you teach them to compare options, make trade-offs, or delay gratification?
* What values do you want to emphasize when they start handling money independently?

TEENAGERS: **Encouraging Autonomy and Mistake-Making**

* How do you support your teen in managing their own money with increasing independence?
* What role do you want to play in helping them open accounts, use a debit card, or manage a part-time job?
* How do you approach mistakes or overspending: with punishment, teaching, or empathy?
* How do you talk about financial ethics (e.g., honesty, giving, consumer choices)?

ADULT CHILDREN: **Supporting Lifelong Financial Learning**

* How do you continue to talk about money in respectful, collaborative ways?
* Are there financial tools or strategies you can offer to help them navigate independence?
* What boundaries do you need around lending, gifting, or shared expenses?
* How can you continue to encourage financial learning without judgment or pressure?

Chapter 4

REIMAGINING GENDER ROLES AND FAMILY STRUCTURES

Parenthood brings us face-to-face with the gender roles and expectations we've internalized from families, culture, religion, and society. For many of us, these expectations come from deeply ingrained "invisible scripts" that have shaped how we think about relationships, responsibilities, and family life. By reimagining these roles, we give ourselves permission to create a dynamic that reflects our values, strengths, and goals, instead of solely the expectations of others.

Understanding the Psychology Behind Gender Roles and Family Expectations

"Invisible scripts" influence everything, from who manages household tasks to how parenting responsibilities are divided, often creating friction when these roles no longer align with modern values or circumstances. Research highlights the impact of traditional gender roles on emotional labor, the often invisible work involved in managing family needs, like remembering doctors' appointments or planning birthday parties. When one partner carries a disproportionate share of this emotional labor, it can lead to resentment or burnout.

Why Reimagining Gender Roles Matters

Challenging and reimagining traditional gender roles helps you honor the values that resonate with you and your partner while releasing those that don't. This process often requires open communication, empathy, and flexibility. By building a dynamic that respects individual contributions and strengths, families can foster an environment where both parents and children thrive.

This chapter explores strategies for redefining roles, balancing emotional labor, and navigating external expectations from family and society. My hope is that these pages will encourage you to craft a family dynamic that is authentic, collaborative, and empowering for everyone involved.

Challenging Traditional Gender Roles

Growing up, my mother was the heart of our home's routines and gatherings. She was the cook, the organizer, the one who made every holiday and birthday feel special. She stayed home with my sister and me for the first handful of years while my father worked to support us. It was the dynamic I'd known and come to expect as "normal" family life, a balance I respected and valued. Naturally, as I got older, I assumed that my own family would follow a similar path, with distinct roles where I might handle the day-to-day needs of our kids and home while my partner focused on bringing home the money to sustain us all. But when my ex-husband and I became parents, it became clear that the traditional roles my parents had modeled didn't fit us as well as we thought they might.

I had a career I loved as a therapist, one that felt important to me beyond just financial reasons, and my ex was just as committed to being present for our children as I was. Honestly, we both wanted "in" on parenting in a way that didn't divide us into separate lanes. That sounded nice in theory, but in practice it meant a lot of messy trial-and-error, who's packing daycare lunches, who's getting up for night wakings, who's taking the afternoon off when a kid is sick. We wanted to build a balance that worked for our strengths and values, not just what we had been taught or expected. This shift led to some challenging but necessary conversations, including one that stands out with my mother. After our first child was born, I was ready to return to work sooner than she'd expected, and she gently questioned my choice. Her concerns were rooted in genuine love and from her own experience of staying home with us for those early years. "Are you sure you're ready?" she asked, adding that her years at home had been essential in her experience as a parent. Her words landed in my chest, part guilt, part defensiveness. I wanted her approval, but I also wanted to trust my gut. I appreciated her perspective and felt grateful for the foundation she gave us, yet I realized that our family was going to have its own, unique balance, a dynamic where both parents would fully engage in raising the kids and nurturing careers, even if it looked different from what we were raised with.

Challenging traditional gender roles used to mean figuring out how to share work, parenting, and emotional labor under one roof. We both worked, traded off daycare drop-offs, and tried to divide responsibilities in a way that felt fair, even when it wasn't perfect. I often carried more of the emotional side, checking in, smoothing things over, and keeping everyone steady, while he took on other roles like managing finances or taking care of the car and home. Since our marriage ended, that balance looks different, but the spirit of it remains. Now, as single parents, we each do it all in our own ways. I'm the one fixing what breaks, taking care of money, and being the loud, playful parent who runs around and is silly. He's the one cooking, tidying, and offering warmth and emotional comfort when our kids need it. Our children get to see both of us stretch beyond old roles, and that's its own kind of radical act showing them that love, care, and capability don't belong to just one parent or one gender.

Resource: In *Fair Play*, Eve Rodsky offers a framework for dividing household responsibilities based on strengths rather than tradition, helping families move toward more balanced, meaningful partnerships.

PRE-CHILD PLANNING: **Exploring Expectations Around Gender Roles**

* What roles did men and women take on in your family growing up, and how did that shape your ideas of parenting?
* What did you learn (directly or indirectly) about who is "supposed" to do what in a household?
* Are there messages about masculinity or femininity that you want to unlearn or rethink before becoming a parent?
* Which traditional roles feel aligned with your values, and which ones feel restrictive or outdated?
* How do you and your partner tend to respond when your values around roles differ from what you were raised with?

DURING PREGNANCY: **Redefining Roles as You Prepare for Parenthood**

* What assumptions are others making about your roles now that pregnancy is visible or public?
* How is the division of emotional and logistical labor shifting as the birth approaches?
* Are you feeling any unspoken pressure to parent in a way that matches your gender, body, or cultural role?
* What kinds of support do both you and your partner need to feel emotionally prepared for parenting?
* How are you handling differing opinions from extended family or your community about who should be doing what?

POSTPARTUM: **Sharing the Load and Rewriting the Script**

* How are responsibilities, both visible and invisible, being divided right now: intentionally or by default?
* Are certain caregiving or household tasks naturally falling to one of you, and why do you think that is?
* What messages do you tell yourself about being "good" at certain roles, and where do those messages come from?
* When you feel unsupported or overwhelmed, how do you bring that up with your partner, and what helps it land?
* How do you feel when others praise or critique how your roles are divided, and what does that stir in you?
* What values do you hope your child learns from watching how you each show up in family life?

TODDLER YEARS: **Maintaining Flexibility as Roles Evolve**

* Are you slipping into old patterns because it's easier, even if they don't feel fair?
* How do your toddler's growing needs highlight the strengths and limits of each partner?
* How do you and your partner show appreciation for the unseen work you each do?
* What messages about gender roles might your toddler already be picking up?
* How can you explain to your toddler that different people can do all types of jobs?

4–8 YEARS: **Teaching Kids About Flexibility and Fairness**

* What do you want your child to believe about gender, work, and fairness?
* How can you show your child that all roles—emotional, practical, paid, unpaid—matter?
* When they ask why mom or dad does certain things, how do you respond?
* What stereotypes are showing up in their books, TV shows, or friend groups?
* How do you want to introduce the idea of equality without relying on shame or guilt?

9–12 YEARS: **Empowering Preteens to Challenge Gender Norms**

* How do you handle it when your child repeats a gender stereotype?
* Are there moments when you've role-modeled going against expectations and talked about it with them?
* How can you involve them in household responsibilities in ways that challenge traditional roles?

* What have they observed in extended family dynamics, and how do you help them make sense of that?
* How do you explain the difference between equality and equity in your family?

TEENAGERS: **Encouraging Teens to Think Critically About Gender Roles**

* How do you talk about fairness in relationships, now and in the future?
* Do you model asking for help and admitting when roles need to shift?
* What cultural or generational expectations are they grappling with?
* How can you prepare your teen for partnership, whether romantic, platonic, or professional, that values mutual respect?
* How do you respond if your teen pushes back on your habits or patterns?

ADULT CHILDREN: **Passing On Values of Equality and Partnership**

* What do you hope your child learned from the way you and your partner shared roles?
* Are there things you wish you'd done differently, and can you talk about that openly?
* How do you respect your adult child's evolving views on family roles, even if they differ from yours?
* What does it look like now to model equality, flexibility, and teamwork in your own relationships?
* How can you celebrate their choices without judgment or subtle correction?

Expanding Conversations About Gender, Identity, and Family Structures

Our family is built from so many different kinds of love and unique stories. Between both sides of our family, we have a blend of same-sex marriages, remarriages, co-parenting after divorce, adoption, and so many varied ways that love and family have come together. It's a gift to be surrounded by such diverse paths to connection, and as our kids grow, we're looking forward to sharing these stories with them in all their richness and honesty. Our family's structure is living proof that love can be strong, resilient, and beautifully varied, and it makes us so grateful to be raising our kids in a time and place where we can be open about this without fear. I know that for my kids, this won't just be theory, it'll be their lived experience of aunties, uncles, cousins, and grandparents who've built families in all kinds of ways.

But that openness isn't something we take for granted, and it's not yet true for everyone. Around the world, and even in our communities, there are children who are bullied, excluded, or harmed simply for being gay, trans, or different in some way. These are real and serious issues. Kids lose their lives to this kind of hatred. It's heavy to even write that as a parent, because the thought of my kids, or anyone's kids, carrying that kind of pain is gutting. I think back to my own upbringing, where certain topics were rarely named, let alone celebrated. For many of us, silence was the default. But now, as parents, we get to decide if silence is something we pass down, or if we want to do it differently.

Whether your child ends up being the one who feels different or the one who's watching how others treat those who are, we all play a part. Are we raising children who know how to lead with compassion? Are we teaching them that love comes in many forms, and that families don't have to follow one script to be real or worthy? Or are we passing down silence and discomfort that leaves room for harm? We can't expect our kids to navigate a world we were never taught to understand without first doing some unlearning ourselves. For me, that unlearning has meant catching moments where I hesitate to explain something, like why two men at the park are holding hands, and choosing to name it with pride instead of awkwardness. It's in the little pauses where our kids learn what we value. That might mean gently stretching past what our parents or grandparents believed. It might mean rethinking how our culture or religion has shaped our views on identity. And it definitely means being willing to listen, learn, and show up in new ways. We hope our children see that each type of relationship and family structure in their world is just another expression of love and commitment. That when people decide to part ways or remarry, it's not a shameful ending but an act of protecting peace and wholeness. That chosen family, the friends and loved ones you lean on, can be just as sacred and life-giving as blood ties. And that identity, whether it's about who you love or how you see yourself, is something to be celebrated, not feared.

Resource: *The Gender Wheel* by Maya Christina Gonzalez is a valuable resource for helping kids understand identity in an open, age-appropriate way, encouraging curiosity and inclusivity.

PRE-CHILD PLANNING: **Laying the Foundation for Inclusivity**

* What beliefs about gender, family roles, or relationships were shaped by your cultural or religious upbringing?
* What assumptions about family structure (e.g., marriage, biological parenting, heterosexual norms) do you want to question or release?

* How do you and your partner feel about raising a child who might identify as LGBTQ+, transgender, nonbinary, or gender-expansive?
* Are there cultural or religious values you want to carry forward, and how can they coexist with affirming all identities and family forms?

DURING PREGNANCY: **Preparing for Conversations About Family and Identity**

* How will you talk about your child's potential identity, including sexual orientation, gender identity, and neurodiversity, with openness and support?
* If your family includes LGBTQ+ members or diverse family structures (e.g., adoption, surrogacy, co-parenting after divorce), how do you plan to talk about these relationships with your child?
* How can you balance cultural or religious expectations with your own evolving values around inclusivity and belonging?
* What community, faith, or cultural traditions can be adapted to support a more expansive view of love and identity?

POSTPARTUM: **Introducing Diversity and Inclusivity Early On**

* How do you want to respond if a family member makes a comment that doesn't align with your inclusive values?
* How are you using language that doesn't assume gender roles or family structures (e.g., "grown-ups" instead of "moms and dads")?

- How are your parenting choices shaped by your own internalized messages around gender and identity?
- Are there affirming communities or resources, faith-based or secular, you can join to support these early conversations?

TODDLER YEARS: **Encouraging Curiosity About Family and Identity**

- How do you begin to explain gender identity, assigned sex at birth, and gender expression to your toddler?
- What do you say when your toddler notices different kinds of families or expressions of gender in public or at daycare?
- When your toddler hears something gendered from a peer or family member (e.g., "only boys like trucks"), how do you respond?
- How can you honor your culture or faith while making room for expansive, affirming conversations about identity?

4–8 YEARS: **Normalizing Conversations About Identity and Family Structures**

- What books or stories can you read together that celebrate LGBTQ+ identities, chosen families, and different cultural traditions?
- How do you explain that some kids may have two moms, two dads, or nonbinary parents and that all families are valid?
- How do you respond when your child asks questions about gender transitions or same-gender relationships?

* How do you help your child understand that love, safety, and respect, not appearance or gender, are what make someone family?

9–12 YEARS: **Encouraging Deeper Conversations About Identity and Inclusivity**

* What media or social situations are influencing your child's beliefs about gender, queerness, or what makes a "normal" family?
* How do you create space for your child to express their own identity, curiosity, or confusion without fear of judgment?
* How do you reconcile differences between your inclusive values and any religious or cultural messages that may conflict with them?

TEENAGERS: **Supporting Teens in Exploring Identity and Inclusivity**

* How do you support your teen in exploring gender identity, pronouns, or sexual orientation in a way that centers safety and affirmation?
* How do you respond when your teen's beliefs challenge your upbringing, religious teachings, or cultural values?
* What LGBTQ+ role models, authors, or community leaders do you share with your teen to show representation and strength?
* How do you navigate extended family dynamics when a teen comes out or asks for their identity to be respected?

ADULT CHILDREN: **Continuing Conversations About Family and Identity**

* How do you continue to affirm your adult child's identity, partnerships, and chosen family structure as they build their own life?
* If your child identifies as LGBTQ+, what does support look like now, in your words, actions, and presence?
* How do you navigate religious or cultural tensions that may arise within your extended family around your child's identity or parenting choices?
* What legacy of inclusion, acceptance, and expansive love do you want to leave behind for your children and their children?

Addressing the Mental Load

The mental load, that constant, invisible checklist that keeps the household running, often falls to one person in a family, even if both partners are equally invested. After we'd finally get the kids to bed and come downstairs, I'd face a long list of tasks that still needed doing: washing dishes, clearing counters, putting away toys, folding laundry, and tidying up. I'd feel the urge to unwind, but there was always more to take care of. Meanwhile, my ex-husband would often settle onto the couch, ready to relax after a long day. With his ADHD, he shifts quickly into relaxation mode, and his "out of sight, out of mind" tendency would kick in—if something wasn't right in front of him, he didn't always notice it. While incredibly supportive, he wasn't seeing the mess and clutter the same way I did, especially after he'd settled in. I'd find myself clattering dishes a little louder than necessary, hoping he'd notice, or lying in bed stewing about how uneven it felt. Then, in the mornings, he'd occasionally make comments about how disorganized things looked or how scattered it all felt, pointing out how it made our routine harder. I knew he didn't mean it critically, but it still stung, as it highlighted how visible the undone tasks were in the daylight. In those moments, I wanted to say, "Do you know why it looks better than it could have? Because I stayed up doing it." His observations came from his own need for order to focus, a need I was trying to meet each night by tackling the tasks alone. One night, after a particularly tiring day, I finally shared with him how heavy it all felt. I explained that, while I understood his need to relax, it was hard for me to wind down with so much still looming over me. It wasn't easy to say out loud, part of me worried I'd sound naggy, but it came out anyway, with tears in my eyes. He listened with his usual warmth, and it became clear that this wasn't just about cleaning, it was about us finding a rhythm that supported us both.

Together, we decided on a "closing tasks" list, similar to what restaurants do at the end of a shift, so we could both feel ready for the next day. The list was simple: wash the dishes, put away toys, wipe down the counters, prep the kids' lunches—enough to feel refreshed in the morning. When we were still together, that list helped us find a sense of teamwork again. We didn't always get it right; there were nights one of us was too tired or times when I felt like I was still doing more, but having something shared made the load feel lighter. Now, living on my own, that list has become mine again, though it feels different these days. There's no one to divide it with, and I've learned to move through it without resentment. Some nights I do it all; other nights I let some rigidity go and choose rest instead if I need to.

Resource: In *Fed Up: Emotional Labor, Women, and the Way Forward*, Gemma Hartley sheds light on the mental load and how to balance it, encouraging families to make the invisible work visible.

PRE-CHILD PLANNING: **Reflecting on Emotional Labor Before Parenthood**

* What messages did you receive growing up about who should manage household tasks or keep track of family needs?
* How did your caregivers divide (or not divide) the mental and emotional labor in your childhood home?
* Which invisible tasks (planning, anticipating, remembering) do you already take on in your partnership, and how do you feel about that balance?
* How do you and your partner each handle planning, multitasking, and anticipating needs?
* What emotions come up when you think about asking for help or setting boundaries around household responsibilities?

DURING PREGNANCY: **Anticipating the Shift in Mental Load**

* What are you noticing about how tasks like scheduling appointments or preparing for the baby are being handled?
* How do you want to handle unspoken expectations about who does what after the baby is born?
* How do you each express appreciation for unseen labor like researching baby products, tracking prenatal milestones, or managing logistics?
* What worries come up when you think about your future role in managing household and parenting tasks?

POSTPARTUM: **Making the Invisible Load Visible**

- ✷ What parts of the mental or emotional load have become more visible, or more overwhelming, since the baby arrived?
- ✷ How are invisible tasks like tracking feedings, planning doctor visits, or anticipating the baby's needs being divided?
- ✷ When do you feel most alone in managing parenting or household responsibilities, and how do you communicate that?
- ✷ How do societal, cultural, or family expectations shape your understanding of who should be "on" and who gets to "rest"?
- ✷ What does rest look like for each of you right now, and is one person sacrificing more to make that happen?

TODDLER YEARS: **Evolving the Mental Load as Needs Grow**

- ✷ How are you managing the increased planning, meals, activities, and tantrum-prevention strategies?
- ✷ Who remembers when the diaper bag needs restocking, or when shoes no longer fit?
- ✷ When one parent is overwhelmed, what signals do you use to tag in or ask for help?
- ✷ How are cultural or generational beliefs shaping who is "supposed to" manage emotional regulation or family organization?

4–8 YEARS: **Balancing Schedules, Responsibilities, and Emotional Labor**

- ✷ How do you and your partner coordinate school events, birthday parties, and extracurriculars?

* Who keeps track of your child's changing emotional needs, friendships, or worries?
* How often do you find yourself reminding others of what needs to happen or preparing things ahead of time without being asked?
* In what ways do your children notice or comment on the division of tasks at home?

9–12 YEARS: **Involving Preteens and Modeling Shared Responsibility**

* Who tracks homework deadlines, permission slips, and special events?
* How are your children being included in family responsibilities, and how do they respond to that?
* What dynamics from your childhood are you noticing being repeated, or shifting, as your child becomes more independent?
* What role do you and your partner each play when it comes to emotional coaching or managing social stressors?

TEENAGERS: **Supporting Independence While Managing the Load**

* How are you and your teen navigating shared responsibilities like household chores or preparing meals?
* Who manages the calendar, rides, appointments, and transitions between school, activities, and downtime?
* When you feel overstretched, how does your family respond?
* What values about balance and partnership do you hope your teen is learning from watching you?

ADULT CHILDREN: **Reflecting on the Legacy of Emotional Labor**

* Looking back, how do you feel about the division of emotional labor over your years of parenting?
* What patterns do you see your adult child repeating or changing in their own life?
* How do you talk with your adult children about the unseen work that went into raising a family?
* What conversations have helped your family appreciate or reimagine the emotional labor passed between generations?

Chapter 5

POSTPARTUM MENTAL HEALTH FOR BOTH PARTNERS

Welcoming a new baby is a profound transition that brings joy and fulfillment, and it can also be an emotional and psychological challenge. Postpartum mental health is shaped by a combination of physical, emotional, and environmental factors that both parents experience in unique ways. Understanding these challenges is essential for navigating this delicate period with empathy and self-awareness.

What Is Postpartum Depression (PPD)?

Postpartum depression is a mood disorder that affects approximately 10 to 20 percent of new mothers but can also impact partners. It goes beyond the "baby blues," which are short-lived feelings of sadness, moodiness, or fatigue that typically resolve within two weeks of birth. PPD is characterized by persistent feelings of sadness, hopelessness, irritability, or disinterest in daily activities. Symptoms may include:

* Intense feelings of guilt or inadequacy.
* Difficulty bonding with the baby.
* Loss of appetite or overeating.
* Insomnia or excessive sleeping.
* Thoughts of self-harm or harming the baby (in severe cases).

PPD is not a sign of weakness or failure; it is a medical condition influenced by hormonal changes, genetic predisposition, and environmental stressors. Early identification and treatment, through therapy, medication, or a combination, can significantly improve outcomes.

What Is Postpartum Anxiety (PPA)?

Postpartum anxiety is another common condition, affecting about 10 to 20 percent of new mothers and up to 20 percent of partners. Unlike PPD, which is marked by feelings of sadness, PPA involves excessive worry, restlessness, and intrusive thoughts. Symptoms might include:

* Racing thoughts or constant worry, especially about the baby's safety or well-being.
* Physical symptoms like a racing heart, stomach discomfort, or dizziness.
* Difficulty relaxing or sleeping, even when the baby is sleeping.
* Avoidance behaviors, such as refusing to leave the baby alone or avoiding social interactions.

Postpartum anxiety often goes unnoticed because it doesn't fit the stereotypical narrative of "sadness" and may even appear as hypervigilance, a quality often celebrated in new parents. However, when worry becomes all-consuming, it can interfere with daily functioning and emotional well-being.

How These Challenges Manifest in Both Parents

For birthing parents, hormonal shifts play a significant role in postpartum mental health. After childbirth, estrogen and progesterone levels plummet, often contributing to mood changes and heightened emotional sensitivity. Physical recovery from childbirth, compounded by the demands of breastfeeding, sleep deprivation, and societal expectations of "perfect parenting," can leave mothers feeling overwhelmed and isolated. For non-birthing parents, postpartum mental health challenges are often rooted in the adjustment to new responsibilities and changing relationship dynamics. Partners may feel pressure to provide emotional and logistical support while navigating their own sleep deprivation, financial stress, or feelings of inadequacy in their parenting role. These emotions are often compounded by the societal stigma that men or non-birthing parents should "just step up," leaving them less likely to seek help.

Trauma and Postpartum Mental Health

Past trauma, whether related to one's upbringing, birth trauma, or previous life events, can significantly influence postpartum mental health. For example:

* A parent with a history of neglect may struggle with feelings of inadequacy or hypervigilance around their baby's care.

* A traumatic birth experience can lead to postpartum PTSD, marked by intrusive thoughts, flashbacks, and difficulty connecting with the baby.
* Childhood experiences of emotional invalidation may resurface, making it harder for a parent to trust their instincts or express their needs.

Acknowledging the role of past trauma in shaping current emotional patterns can provide a pathway to healing and deeper connection with both oneself and one's family.

Supporting Postpartum Mental Health for Both Parents

In this chapter, we'll dive into the emotional complexities of the postpartum period for both parents, addressing issues like postpartum rage, guilt, anxiety, and changes in identity. We'll provide tools to recognize signs of distress, foster open communication, and build systems of mutual support. In exploring age-specific challenges from the postpartum phase to the toddler years and beyond, you'll find prompts tailored to every stage of your parenting journey.

Parenting is inherently demanding, but for those working to stop cycles of trauma or navigating unique mental health challenges, it can feel even heavier. Through self-awareness, compassion, and actionable tools, this chapter aims to empower you to show up for your family and yourself with recognition and love.

Recognizing Postpartum Mental Health Challenges

Adjusting to life with a new baby is emotionally intense, and I remember not feeling a big shift until after our second child came into our lives. About six months after my daughter was born, when my son was two, I noticed a change in myself that I couldn't shake. I was no longer feeling that natural excitement about things, and the usual daily tasks suddenly felt heavier. My mood was persistently low, and it was as if the color had drained out of life. I struggled to think of things to look forward to or to get excited about; everything felt muted, harder to reach. I remember sitting on the floor with my kids, building blocks with them, and feeling flat inside, going through the motions but not really feeling joy. That scared me. I was also more tired than usual, and my energy to get through each day seemed lower than ever. After weeks of pushing through, I finally shared what I was feeling with my friends and family, and in particular, with my sister, who gently suggested that this might be more than just regular fatigue; it could be postpartum depression, even if it had shown up so far after birth. Up until then, I'd kept telling myself, "It's just the sleep deprivation ... it'll pass," but hearing her name it made me realize I couldn't just push it away. That conversation was a wake-up call, a reminder that postpartum mental health changes can surface at any time, even many months after birth. It forced me to step back and reflect on what I'd stopped doing to care for myself outside of being a mom, wife, and a therapist, and I realized just how much I had let go of things that once brought me joy and fulfillment.

I reached out for support, and with guidance, I started taking small steps to reconnect with myself. One of those was signing up for a gym membership and setting a time to go after daycare drop-off for my son and before work. This felt almost like a guilty indulgence at first. Finding an hour in the day for myself seemed impossible, and the "mom guilt" of taking that time weighed on me. I remember driving there the first week and almost turning around because I felt selfish. But I forced myself to walk in. Getting into that new routine helped more than I could've anticipated. With the exercise, I felt a surge in energy and a lift in my mood, those endorphins reminding me of who I was outside my roles. I also made a point to check in regularly with friends, open up more to my husband, and bring in more wholesome foods at home. Some days I would still feel back in survival mode, cereal for dinner, unanswered texts, skipping the gym, but even those small steps added up over time. Together, these small changes made a huge difference, and gradually, I felt myself returning to a place of stability and joy. This whole season reminded me that postpartum mental health doesn't follow a neat timeline. Just because you're months out of the newborn stage doesn't mean you're "safe" from depression or anxiety. It can sneak up when you least expect it. By acknowledging the need for self-care and seeking the right support, I found a way back to myself, realizing just how essential these small acts are for navigating the complex journey of parenthood.

As time has passed, I've learned how important it is to care for my own mental health while recognizing that fathers and co-parents can struggle too. Even though my ex-husband and I now live in separate homes, I still think about how fatherhood affects him, how different, yet equally real, his emotional load can be. When we were together, I often initiated the deeper conversations about feelings, but I could see that he also wrestled quietly with questions about whether he was doing enough or being the kind of dad he hoped to be. I think many men experience that silently, without the same language or space to name it. I also noticed how most of his friendships leaned toward humor and lightness, while my girlfriends and I often talked about how emotionally draining motherhood could be and validated each other's experiences regularly. Those conversations helped us feel seen and understood in a way I'm not sure he always had access to. Now, as co-parents, we each have our own ways of coping, growing, and finding steadiness for our kids. I've come to see that postpartum mental health is a family story. When either parent struggles, it ripples through everyone. And when either of us takes care of ourselves, it strengthens the whole family. Watching him navigate fatherhood in his own way, and giving myself permission to do the same, has reminded me that healing and growth, for both of us, matter deeply.

Resource: Mark Williams's *Daddy Blues* shares his personal experience of postnatal depression, shedding light on how it can affect fathers as well as mothers. In the early days of parenthood, he felt overwhelmed by the challenges of caring for a newborn and the emotional distance in his relationship. Not realizing that men could also face postpartum depression, he found himself isolated and eventually turned to alcohol as a way to cope. The book follows his journey through this difficult period, offering an honest look at the impact of paternal mental health struggles.

PRE-CHILD PLANNING: **Preparing for Emotional Shifts in Parenthood**

* What emotions do you anticipate might come up as you adjust to parenthood?
* How do you or your partner handle stress, and how might those responses change with the added demands of a baby?
* How did your parents or caregivers respond to emotional overwhelm growing up? How might that influence your approach now?
* Who in your support network, including friends, family, or professionals, can you imagine turning to for emotional support once the baby arrives?

* What conversations do you need to have with extended family about the mental health challenges that can arise in early parenthood?

DURING PREGNANCY: **Building Awareness of Postpartum Mental Health**

* What surprising feelings have surfaced during pregnancy, and how might they shift postpartum?
* How can you recognize early signs of postpartum anxiety or depression in yourself or your partner?
* How do your family and friends talk about mental health? Is it something that feels safe to bring up with them?
* Who could check in on you during the postpartum period, not just about the baby, but about how you're doing emotionally?
* What would make it easier to ask for help or say "I'm struggling" to someone in your circle?

POSTPARTUM: **Honoring the Emotional Landscape of the First Year**

* What emotions have surfaced for you since your baby arrived, and how are they affecting your day-to-day life?
* How has sleep deprivation impacted your ability to care for yourself, your partner, and your baby emotionally?
* How can you ask for support when you feel overwhelmed, whether that's with the baby or just having someone check in with you?
* Who has made you feel truly supported during this time, and what did they do that helped?

* What makes it easier, or harder, for you to be honest with loved ones about how you're really doing?
* Who can you turn to when you need a break, and what kind of support would actually feel restorative?

TODDLER YEARS: **Recognizing Long-Term Postpartum Mental Health Challenges**

* Are there lingering feelings of anxiety, disconnection, or low mood that haven't fully lifted?
* What old coping strategies are no longer serving you, and what new ones could support you better?
* Who in your life do you feel truly gets how draining this season of parenting can be?
* How do you talk about your emotional needs with family or friends when they assume things have gotten "easier"?
* How can your parenting community (other parents, daycare staff, friends) help you feel seen during tough days?

4–8 YEARS: **Reflecting on Early Parenting's Emotional Impact**

* How do you reflect on the mental health challenges you faced in the early years of parenting?
* How do you model self-care and emotional awareness for your child now?
* What role did your family or friends play in your early parenting experience, and what did you need more or less of?
* Have you talked with others in your parenting circle about those first few years? What helped or hurt?

* What practices (journaling, therapy, movement, creative expression) are helping you continue to process your experience?

9–12 YEARS: **Modeling Mental Health Awareness for Older Children**

* How do you model emotional resilience and self-compassion in front of your preteen?
* What parts of your mental health journey do you feel safe sharing with your child to help normalize the topic?
* How do you and your partner, or parenting team, check in with each other about emotional well-being now? How has your support system evolved, and who continues to show up for you in meaningful ways? What conversations about mental health are you ready to have with your child, and what might you still be holding back?

TEENAGERS: **Supporting Each Other While Parenting Teens**

* How do you and your partner navigate emotional challenges now that your children are older?
* When was the last time you talked openly with a friend or family member about your mental health as a parent?
* What would your teen say they've learned from watching you manage stress or emotional pain?
* What practices still help you feel grounded or supported? Which ones no longer do?
* How do you encourage your teen to care for their mental health without projecting your past struggles onto them?

ADULT CHILDREN: **Reflecting on Your Mental Health Journey as Parents**

* How has your experience with postpartum or parenting-related mental health shaped who you are today?
* What lessons about emotional resilience do you hope to pass on to your adult children?
* What parts of your early parenting story do you wish you'd shared more openly with family or friends at the time?
* How do you want your children to remember your approach to mental health and emotional care?
* What practices or conversations are still part of your life to nurture your emotional well-being now?

Navigating Postpartum Rage

For many parents, the emotional demands of new parenthood bring unexpected feelings, including anger and frustration. As someone with ADHD diagnosed later in life, I've come to understand just how much my brain's reactivity, sensitivity to noise, and difficulty regulating emotions can impact the way I show up as a mom. Even with medication, it's not always easy. And on the days I forget to take it, I can feel everything rising closer to the surface—faster, louder, and harder to manage.

One evening, not long ago, both of my kids were in the bath. My son was playing with a toy and gently bumped his little sister with it. She said "no," clearly. A moment later, he did it again (the bath was small; the bump was unintentional, but still made an impact). She started to cry. And before I could even think, I snapped. I raised my voice, sharply, too loud, and yelled, "Stop touching her!" as I moved his arm away abruptly. It wasn't a calm boundary;

it was an eruption. My chest was hot, my heart pounding, my hands shaking, and for a second, it felt like I wasn't even in control of my own voice. As soon as the words left my mouth, I saw it. The way my son's face changed. His eyes dropped. His shoulders sank. His expression folded into something that looked like a mix of sadness and fear, and he started to cry. I had scared him. Not because I meant to, but because my nervous system was already running on fumes, and in that moment, I just didn't have the buffer. The shame hit instantly, the "what kind of mom does that?" voice creeping in before I even had a chance to breathe. I took a breath. Then another. I crouched down beside the tub and softened my voice: "That scared you. I can see that. I'm sorry I yelled." I pulled him into a towel-wrapped hug, grounding us both. "You're not in trouble. I just got overwhelmed hearing your sister cry and didn't handle it the way I wanted to."

Behind that raised voice was a mom who had forgotten to take her ADHD medication that day. A mom who hadn't had a quiet moment. A mom who felt like she couldn't handle one more sound. One more splash. One more cry. In that moment, my rage didn't feel logical or measured; it felt primal, like my body was hijacked by the desperate need to shut everything down. That wasn't about him. It was about me, my overstimulation, my dysregulation, and my very human limits. Moments like that have taught me so much about self-compassion and the importance of being with my kids in their emotions first instead of bulldozing them with mine unintentionally. My anger wasn't just anger—it was noise sensitivity, it was fear that my daughter might get hurt, it was shame bubbling up for not staying calm, and it was exhaustion from the invisible labor I carry. That's what postpartum rage has felt like for me: sudden, overwhelming, disproportionate, the kind of reaction that leaves you shaky and flooded with guilt after. Postpartum rage, especially with ADHD, doesn't mean you're a bad parent; it means you're an overstimulated and overwhelmed one. And I'm learning that recognizing these moments, not hiding from them, is part of how I repair, grow, and stay connected to my kids and to myself. Some nights I still replay the look on my son's face, and it breaks me, but repair has become my way forward, reminding both him and myself that love and connection don't vanish because of one hard moment.

Resource: *Motherhood: Facing and Finding Yourself* by Lisa Marchiano dives into the transformative challenges of early parenthood, exploring how new parents can navigate complex emotions like anger, frustration, and even guilt. Marchiano uses real-life stories and psychological insights to help parents understand the root of these intense feelings, encouraging self-compassion and personal growth. It's an insightful guide for recognizing difficult emotions as part of the natural transformation into parenthood rather than as personal failures.

PRE-CHILD PLANNING: **Anticipating Emotional Challenges of Parenthood**

- How do you currently manage feelings of frustration or anger, and how might these responses change when you're sleep-deprived or overstimulated?
- What triggers tend to escalate your emotions, and how might these show up in early parenting?
- What have you learned from your family or upbringing about how anger is expressed or suppressed?
- Who in your life can you speak to about emotional regulation without feeling judged: friends, siblings, or mentors?

- How can you involve your wider circle (e.g., in-laws, doulas, friends) in conversations about emotional support after the baby arrives?

DURING PREGNANCY: **Preparing for Emotional Intensity**

- What current stressors seem to spark irritability or tension, and how might they increase after the baby arrives?
- How do you and your partner currently resolve conflict, and what might need to change to stay connected under pressure?
- Who in your extended family tends to help you feel calmer or more reactive? What boundaries might be needed?
- What kind of support would you want from others when you're feeling emotionally overwhelmed?
- How can you start discussing with grandparents, friends, or siblings the importance of being there for you emotionally, not just for the baby?

POSTPARTUM: **Making Space for Big Emotions**

- What moments of anger, irritation, or resentment have surprised you since becoming a parent, and what might those feelings be trying to tell you?
- How do you express frustration or overwhelm to your partner or family without guilt or shame, and what makes that easier or harder?
- How safe do you feel sharing your intense emotions with people close to you, and how have they responded when you've been struggling?

* What helps you recover from an emotional outburst, and who can you lean on afterward for validation or grounding?
* What conversations do you need to have with your inner circle to feel supported without being dismissed, minimized, or judged?
* Who in your life seems to understand your capacity limits without needing a long explanation, and how can you keep them close?

TODDLER YEARS: **Managing Emotional Outbursts in the Busy Toddler Stage**

* How do you catch yourself when you're about to lose your temper, and what helps you ground in those moments?
* Who do you feel safe calling or texting after a meltdown or hard parenting day?
* What boundaries need to be reevaluated with family or caregivers who may unintentionally increase your stress?
* How do you want to talk about anger in your home, with your partner, with your child, and with your extended family?
* What kind of support do you wish others offered when you're clearly "at your limit"?

4–8 YEARS: **Reflecting on Emotional Growth**

* How do you explain emotional outbursts to your child now, and what language helps them understand it's not their fault?
* What memories do you carry from earlier parenting years when your anger felt out of control? How have you made peace with them?

* What does your family or community expect of you emotionally now, and what's changed in your boundaries?
* How do you ask for space when you need to cool down, and how does your child respond?
* What would you want your child to know about what anger means, and doesn't mean, about being a parent?

9–12 YEARS: **Teaching Emotional Awareness to Preteens**

* How has your emotional regulation changed over the years, and what helped you grow?
* What stories or insights from the early parenting years can you share with your child to help normalize strong emotions?
* How do you model repair after an outburst, with your child, your partner, or others?
* What roles do grandparents or extended family play in your emotional landscape now? Do they offer support or still expect emotional labor from you?
* How do you show your child that asking for help with emotions is a strength, not a weakness?

TEENAGERS: **Modeling Emotional Balance for Teens**

* What do you wish your teen understood about how hard those early years of parenting were for your mental health?
* How do you model healthy conflict and repair with your partner in front of your teen?
* What language or gestures help you name your emotions before they turn into outbursts now?

- What kind of emotional support do you still need from your community, and how do you seek it out?
- How do you hold space for both your teen's big emotions and your own?

ADULT CHILDREN: **Reflecting on Emotional Growth as Parents**

- What moments of emotional struggle in early parenting do you still carry, and what healing has taken place?
- What would you want your adult children to know about how you coped with anger or rage as a new parent?
- How can you talk honestly about the challenges of early parenting without feeling shame?
- How have your relationships with your partner, friends, or extended family changed as a result of these emotional experiences?
- What emotional wisdom do you now carry that you wish you had known at the start?

Fostering Emotional Intelligence and Mental Health Awareness in Children

We're part of a generation that is prioritizing emotional and mental health awareness for our kids, hoping they grow up with tools that many of us didn't have. There was one day that really drove this home for me, a day when my toddler was having a particularly tough time. The morning had been full of small frustrations, and by the time he was trying to play with his favorite toy car, which wouldn't roll down the ramp as he'd wanted, he reached his limit. He began to melt down, frustrated tears streaming down his cheeks as his cries grew louder. Watching him, I felt that familiar tug, the instinct to "fix" it, to say something soothing or distracting just to make it all better. Seeing his little face so scrunched up in frustration brought out a deep urge in me to take away his discomfort. Part of me wanted to grab the toy, show him how to line it up, or even swap it out for something else just to stop the crying. But something stopped me, and I paused. Instead of jumping in to solve it, I knelt beside him, took a breath, and resisted the impulse to "make it right." Instead, I looked into his teary eyes and said, "I see you're feeling really frustrated right now, buddy. Your car isn't going down the way you wanted it to, and that's hard." For a moment, he just looked at me, as if I'd spoken some magic words he didn't expect. His cries softened, and I could see his little shoulders relax just a bit and he said, "Yeah, it's not working properly and I need help." I could tell he felt understood. I hadn't fixed the car, but I had given him something he needed even more: validation. For him, it was a small yet meaningful moment, someone acknowledging his frustration without trying to change it or brush it away. And for me, it was a wake-up call that maybe I could try this approach with myself too. I realized how often I rush to shut down my own feelings with "It's fine" or "I don't have time for this," when maybe what I need is the same pause and acknowledgment I had just given him.

That moment showed me that teaching emotional intelligence takes practice, and sometimes it starts with practicing on ourselves. As I sat there with my son, I realized that I wanted something different for him than what so many of us grew up with. I wanted him to feel that his emotions, whether frustration, sadness, or anger, were valid and that he didn't need to hide them or make them smaller. I don't always get it right; sometimes I still snap or rush him through his big feelings, but I'm trying. In showing him that his feelings are okay, I'm slowly learning to give myself the same permission, creating space for both of us to express ourselves openly.

Resource: *The Whole-Brain Child* by Dr. Daniel Siegel and Dr. Tina Payne Bryson introduces age-appropriate techniques for helping children understand and manage their emotions. It emphasizes the importance of nurturing mental health skills from a young age, which benefits both children and parents.

PRE-CHILD PLANNING: **Building a Foundation for Emotional Awareness**

- How were emotions handled in your family growing up? Were feelings talked about, dismissed, or avoided?
- Which emotional habits or coping strategies, both helpful and unhelpful, did you learn from your caregivers?
- How did your caregivers respond when you were upset, afraid, or angry? How do you feel about those responses now?
- In what ways do you want your child's emotional experience to be similar to or different from your own?
- Are there trusted friends or family members you feel comfortable talking to about your intentions around emotional parenting?

DURING PREGNANCY: **Preparing to Model Emotional Intelligence**

- How do you and your partner currently talk about emotions, and what kind of emotional environment do you hope to create once your baby arrives?

* What books or resources are you exploring during pregnancy to help guide how you'll talk about and model emotions?
* What emotional language or phrases do you want to practice now so they feel natural in your parenting later on (e.g., "It's okay to feel sad," "You're allowed to be upset")?
* Who in your family or close circle might benefit from learning more about responding to children's emotions with validation and empathy?
* Are there early conversations you want to start with grandparents, aunts/uncles, or chosen family about your intentions around emotional development and what kind of support you'll need?

POSTPARTUM: **Building Emotional Awareness from Day One**

* How do you manage your emotional highs and lows during the postpartum period, and what helps you stay grounded?
* How do you respond to your baby's distress, and what might they be learning from your tone, body language, or presence?
* What kind of response from visitors, family, or caregivers feels most supportive when your baby is upset?
* What kinds of emotional language are you using at home, even if your baby doesn't yet understand the words?
* Have you discussed with family or friends using validating phrases with your baby, such as "That was hard" or "I see you're upset"?

* How can your community support an environment where emotional expression is welcomed, not rushed, silenced, or minimized?

TODDLER YEARS: **Building Emotional Awareness Through Validation**

* How do you name your toddler's feelings in the moment to help them understand what they're experiencing?
* What tools (emotion charts, storybooks, calming corners) have been most helpful in supporting your toddler's emotional growth?
* How do your child's other caregivers (e.g., daycare staff, grandparents) approach emotional outbursts?
* Have you discussed with family or friends what language feels aligned with your parenting approach during big feelings?
* How do you navigate unsolicited advice about "disciplining" emotions, especially from well-meaning relatives?

4–8 YEARS: **Teaching Empathy and Perspective-Taking**

* How do you help your child imagine how others might feel in different situations?
* What stories or books have sparked good conversations about empathy or big emotions?
* How does your child express emotions in front of other family members? Do they feel safe or guarded?
* How can you engage grandparents or other adults in teaching empathy and emotional vocabulary?

* How do you respond when someone else downplays your child's emotions in front of them?

9–12 YEARS: **Strengthening Emotional Tools for Preteens**

* How do you support your preteen when they're emotionally overwhelmed or withdrawn?
* What emotional habits or tools (like journaling, mindfulness, peer support) are they developing?
* How involved is your community (e.g., teachers, coaches, family) in reinforcing emotional awareness?
* Have you had conversations with extended family about respecting emotional boundaries (like privacy, space, or autonomy)?
* How can you model repair if a family member invalidates your child's emotions?

TEENAGERS: **Encouraging Emotional Resilience and Awareness in Teens**

* How do you create a home environment where your teen feels emotionally safe and respected?
* How do you guide your teen to recognize when someone else may need emotional support or care?
* What mental health language or practices have you shared with your teen so far?
* How do your teen's relationships with extended family affect their sense of emotional safety?
* Have you invited your community into mental health conversations, or are there still barriers?

ADULT CHILDREN: **Reflecting on Emotional Intelligence and Mental Health Awareness**

* What emotional tools or lessons do you see your adult child using in their own life?
* How have conversations about mental health evolved in your family over the years?
* Are there stories from your early parenting years that could normalize struggle or emotional growth for your child now?
* How do you continue modeling emotional intelligence for your adult children and the next generation?
* What are you still learning about emotional health that you'd want to share with your family openly?

Chapter 6

ENHANCING INTIMACY AND CONNECTION POST-BABY

When a baby enters the picture, everything about life shifts, including the way we connect with our partners. Quiet, uninterrupted time together turns into a series of feedings, diaper changes, and the kind of exhaustion that leaves little room for romance. For many couples, intimacy and closeness take a backseat to the practical demands of parenting. The reality is that the postpartum period often brings intense adjustments, making reconnection feel like a challenge rather than a natural continuation of your relationship. This chapter is about rediscovering intimacy and nurturing a sense of closeness, even when time and energy are limited. Rebuilding connection post-baby goes beyond physical intimacy and involves finding new ways to foster emotional closeness and rekindle the bond that brought you together in the first place.

The Psychological Shifts in Intimacy and Connection After Baby

From a psychological perspective, the postpartum period introduces significant changes in identity, routine, and relationship dynamics, all of which influence intimacy. Couples often find themselves navigating what psychologists call the "dual identity" of parenthood: simultaneously being a caregiver and a partner. This duality can create tension, as parents shift between roles and struggle to find time for connection. Maybe you have more demands and opinions of how the other person is parenting or caring for your child. Maybe you had a disagreement over how to discipline and due to a lack of conflict-resolution skills, you now harbor resentment and don't feel heard or comfortable opening up with your partner anymore.

Physical changes, particularly for the birthing parent, also affect intimacy. Postpartum recovery often involves shifts in body image, physical comfort, and self-awareness, which can influence how partners engage in physical and emotional closeness. Studies suggest that open communication and mutual patience are critical for navigating these changes, as they allow partners to adapt to their new dynamic without pressure or misunderstanding.

Why Rebuilding Intimacy Matters

Rebuilding intimacy after becoming parents is key to building a strong, supportive partnership. While physical closeness matters, emotional intimacy often becomes even more important as couples turn to each other for comfort and connection. Simple, intentional gestures, like sharing a moment of gratitude or holding hands on a walk, can help bring back a sense of closeness and stability during this big transition. When intimacy is nurtured, it strengthens your relationship and creates a space where both partners feel seen and supported. When it isn't prioritized, though, distance can grow. Over time, this can lead to feelings of isolation, resentment, anger, and disconnection. You may find yourself drifting further from your partner, unsure how to name what you're feeling and tempted to seek happiness, excitement, or connection outside the relationship instead of rebuilding it together.

In this chapter, we'll explore how to nurture intimacy and connection across different stages of parenting, focusing on practical strategies to navigate physical and emotional changes. By the end, I hope you'll feel equipped to redefine intimacy in ways that honor your evolving relationship and strengthen your bond.

Understanding Physical Changes Post-Baby

Physical changes after birth can bring up a complex mix of feelings about comfort, identity, and body image. After my first child was born, I remember feeling so out of touch with my body. It wasn't just the way I looked; it was how I felt inside my own skin. Parts of me felt completely foreign, some areas overly sensitive, others oddly numb, like I was disconnected from myself. I knew exactly what my body had looked like for decades of my life, and all of a sudden it had changed so drastically over the past nine months, and again postpartum. I had anticipated some discomfort, sure, but I hadn't expected this lingering sense of alienation. I remember one evening a few weeks after the birth, exhausted but finally settling into bed with a faint sense of relief. My husband reached out to hold me; his touch felt gentle and familiar. But even that simple touch made my whole body tense up, as though I was a stranger to both him and myself. I could feel his confusion, his worry that maybe he'd done something wrong. And there I was, stuck between guilt for pulling away and resentment that I couldn't just enjoy it or get into it so easily like before. I tried to relax, to melt into the touch like I had before, but everything felt different, almost too much, like my skin was overly thin, or my senses too raw to handle closeness. I lay there, conflicted between wanting the comfort of that embrace and feeling that it was somehow overwhelming. I had to explain to him that I wasn't sure what I was feeling, that I just needed space. Saying those words out loud felt clumsy, like I was breaking something between us, even though I knew I needed that boundary. It was such an isolating experience, to feel this way in a body that had carried life, a body that was supposed to bring me joy and pride. But there I was, feeling more like a vessel that had outlived its purpose than the person I used to be.

Over the next few weeks, I struggled to reconcile this sense of disconnection. I would catch glimpses of myself in the mirror, sometimes barely recognizing my reflection. Every physical change—a scar, a new softness, the tenderness in places I'd never noticed—felt like a reminder of how much I'd given up both physically and emotionally. Sometimes I'd stare at old photos of myself and wonder if I'd ever feel at home in my body again, not because I needed to "bounce back," but because I missed the feeling of ease and familiarity. And though my husband at the time was incredibly supportive, always gentle and understanding, I knew he couldn't ever fully understand what was going on with me. Healing wasn't linear, and it wasn't just about stitches and scars closing. It was about slowly figuring out who I was in this body, how to live in it, and how to let it be enough. For me, it was about rediscovering myself in a body that felt foreign, adjusting to new sensations, learning new boundaries, and, ultimately, accepting that intimacy might look different for a while. And that was okay, it just took time to accept that this journey would be slow, that feeling "like myself" again was a process, and that my partner and I would have to navigate it with patience, compassion, and understanding.

Resources: In *The Fourth Trimester* by Kimberly Ann Johnson and *Come as You Are* by Emily Nagoski, parents are offered compassionate guidance for understanding the body's physical and emotional needs, and how this changes post-baby. These resources emphasize moving at your own pace, focusing on self-compassion, and reclaiming comfort and body awareness.

PRE-CHILD PLANNING: **Preparing for Physical and Emotional Changes After Birth**

* What messages did you grow up with about bodies, appearance, or physical affection, especially after major life changes like childbirth?
* How do you imagine your body or your partner's body might change after birth? What emotions or expectations do you carry around that?
* What beliefs do you hold around touch, intimacy, and recovery, and where did they come from?
* How can you both approach postpartum recovery with patience, curiosity, and compassion?
* What boundaries or forms of physical support might feel helpful (or unhelpful) to either of you?
* How do you want family members or friends to talk about appearance, bodies, or touch during the postpartum phase?

DURING PREGNANCY: **Anticipating Changes and Building Awareness**

* What has it been like for you to experience (or witness in your pregnant partner) the physical changes that come with pregnancy?

* How might your views on intimacy, comfort, or attraction shift as your body or your partner's body changes?
* What conversations can you start now about physical boundaries, emotional check-ins, and mutual care postpartum?
* How can you begin to create a shared language for expressing discomfort, desire, or emotional distance without shame or pressure?
* Are there beliefs or expectations from family, culture, or media that feel worth questioning?

POSTPARTUM: **Honoring the Body's Recovery and Redefining Closeness**

* What physical and emotional changes have you noticed since birth, and how do you name or make space for those together?
* What kinds of touch feel comforting, overwhelming, or off-limits right now, and how can you talk about that without guilt or pressure?
* How do the roles of caregiving, exhaustion, and constant physical demand affect your sense of body autonomy or connection?
* How do you support each other's boundaries without taking them personally or rushing the healing process?
* What has helped you (or your partner) feel more grounded or connected in your body during this first year?
* Are there outside messages, from media, family, or friends, that add pressure or shame to your healing process, and how can you protect yourselves from that?

TODDLER YEARS: **Adjusting Expectations and Prioritizing Comfort**

* For both you and your partner, what's shifted physically or emotionally in your relationship to your body or each other's bodies since early postpartum?
* How do you each define comfort now, whether that means intimacy, relaxation, rest, or play?
* How do you communicate about what's changed and what you need physically from each other with curiosity rather than comparison?
* How are you helping one another carry the load of physical and emotional labor at this stage?

4–8 YEARS: **Reclaiming Comfort and Confidence in Your Body**

* How has your self-image evolved in the years since becoming a parent? How does your partner reflect or support that journey?
* How do you each define "feeling good in your body" now, and how do you make time or space for that?
* Are there differences in how you each approach self-care or physical comfort? How can you support one another without judgment?
* How do you talk about your body in front of your child, and what values are they absorbing from those moments?
* In what ways are you helping your child understand that bodies change, grow, and still deserve care and respect?

9–12 YEARS: **Reflecting on and Celebrating Your Body's Journey**

- How do you show your child that bodies are worthy of respect regardless of shape, ability, or history?
- How do you and your partner feel about your physical and emotional self now, and how are those feelings shaped by parenting?
- Are there ways you want to reconnect with yourself physically, whether through touch, movement, or rest?
- How do you balance physical self-care with the growing demands of this stage of parenting?
- What are you teaching your child, directly or indirectly, about respecting their own and others' physical boundaries?

TEENAGERS: **Teaching Body Awareness and Acceptance to Teens**

- What do you want your teen to understand about how bodies change through different seasons of life?
- How do you model self-acceptance and care in the way you talk about or treat your body, and your partner's?
- Are there conversations you've had (or want to have) with your teen about boundaries, consent, and respect in relationships?
- How do you support one another when body image insecurities or physical exhaustion resurface?
- What do you hope your teen learns from watching how you navigate closeness, discomfort, and self-compassion?

ADULT CHILDREN: **Reflecting on Physical and Emotional Growth as a Parent**

* When you reflect on the journey your body has taken since becoming a parent, what stands out? What has changed in how you view yourself?
* What lessons about body image, resilience, and healing do you want your adult children to carry forward?
* How has your partnership (or your relationship with self) grown in understanding each other's physical and emotional needs over time?
* How do you still honor your body's needs, changes, or limitations, even years after early parenting has passed?
* In what ways are you continuing to grow in self-awareness, and how do you want to share that growth with your adult children or broader community?

Balancing Physical and Emotional Needs

Before kids, intimacy often comes naturally. You and your partner have more time, long conversations, spontaneous dates, slow mornings, and space to explore who you are as individuals and as a couple. Physical connection, emotional closeness, and fun flow easily. You can really see each other and show up with presence, which can help you feel connected in all kinds of ways, from sex to laughter to late-night talks.

After becoming parents, that version of your relationship may start to shift, slowly at first, and then all at once. Your time together likely becomes more functional. Conversations that used to be about dreams or ideas turn into checklists: naps, feeding schedules, groceries.

Requests become logistical, "Can you switch the laundry?" "Can you grab the bottle?" You might even find yourself "teaching" your partner about parenting instead of connecting emotionally, like you've slipped into the role of a coach instead of a teammate. The dynamic can feel jarring. You're stretched thin, and intimacy starts to feel like something you have to plan rather than something that simply happens.

Finding your way back to each other in this season takes conscious intention. Sometimes it means planning a date night weeks in advance, even if it takes a spreadsheet and a babysitter to make it happen. And sometimes those nights end in exhaustion or small talk about the kids, and that's okay. Just sitting across from each other without little hands tugging at you can feel like a reset. Those quiet moments help you remember who you were before parenting became the main job description, and to reconnect without the constant noise of responsibility.

Intimacy also changes shape. Sometimes it's not about sex, but about a lingering hug in the kitchen, watching a show together without your phones, or sending a text during the day that isn't about logistics but about connection. These small gestures matter. Some weeks, that's all you can manage, and that doesn't mean something's wrong; it just means life is full. You might also start to notice how quickly defensiveness shows up when either of you feels hurt. Learning to validate each other, to take accountability without blame, becomes essential. It's not easy. There will be nights when you both shut down or sulk instead of talking it through. But coming back to the table, even imperfectly, builds safety and trust over time.

It's also normal for physical intimacy to feel complicated after kids. If sex has been your main way to express closeness, and suddenly it's less frequent, it's easy to feel anxious, disconnected, or even rejected. You might wonder if your partner still finds you attractive or if the spark is gone. And your partner might be wondering the same thing but not saying it out loud. The truth is, this stage of life takes a toll on closeness. It asks for more patience, more creativity, and more honesty than before. But there's still room to choose tenderness, to find small ways to say, "I still see you. I still care."

Resource: *And Baby Makes Three* by Drs. John and Julie Gottman explore how to build connection and intimacy post-baby. The book provides insights into nurturing emotional closeness, patience, and self-compassion, even when physical energy is low.

PRE-CHILD PLANNING: **Preparing for Emotional and Physical Adjustments in Parenthood**

* Growing up, what did you observe in your family around emotional closeness, physical affection, and stress?
* How do you want to show appreciation and connection to your partner, and how can you also build connection with your support system?
* Who in your life (family, friends, chosen family) do you imagine leaning on emotionally or practically once the baby arrives?
* How might your expectations around emotional closeness shift with the arrival of a baby? Have you talked about this with your partner or close family?
* What boundaries or communication strategies might be helpful with in-laws or relatives who want to be involved in early parenting?

DURING PREGNANCY: **Building Connection Amid Physical and Emotional Changes**

- What forms of emotional support feel most nourishing right now, and who in your circle has been able to offer that?
- How do you and your partner express closeness in ways that feel realistic with your current energy levels?
- What kinds of check-ins or shared rituals could you start now that might carry into early parenthood?
- How have your friends or extended family responded to your pregnancy so far, and how do you want to set the tone for ongoing involvement?
- Are there gentle ways you can ask for help or name what's emotionally challenging with those close to you?

POSTPARTUM: **Redefining Connection and Support in Early Parenthood**

- What kinds of emotional or physical closeness from your partner feel most supportive right now, and how can you communicate those needs?
- What small gestures (from your partner, family, or community) help you feel seen and less alone during this season?
- How do you protect small moments of connection, even if it's just five minutes, in the midst of long and tiring days?
- Who can you be emotionally honest with about how you're really doing, physically, mentally, or emotionally?

* Are there people who drain your energy right now, and what boundaries might help protect your emotional bandwidth?
* What's one way someone in your "village" could show up for you this week, practically or emotionally?

TODDLER YEARS: **Balancing the Demands of Toddlers with Emotional Connection**

* How can you and your partner share appreciation, even when tension is high and sleep is low?
* What kinds of emotional support do you need from others beyond your partner, and who has shown up well for you?
* What does "feeling connected" mean to you these days, and who in your circle offers that feeling?
* How do you manage expectations from extended family about how involved they are or how you parent?
* Are there ways to create moments of joy or lightness, alone, with your partner, or with friends, that remind you of who you are outside of parenting?

4–8 YEARS: **Strengthening Your Bond During School-Age Parenting**

* What routines, with your partner or as a family, help you feel more emotionally aligned?
* Are you open with close friends or relatives about the toll parenting can take on your connection and energy?
* What helps you and your partner repair after conflict or disconnection?

* How can you model kindness, respect, and emotional patience in your family system?
* Are there ways your extended family could support you more effectively or ways to gently communicate what's not working?

9–12 YEARS: **Modeling Connection and Patience for Preteens**

* How do you show emotional connection in front of your preteen, and how do they respond to it?
* What shared activities bring you and your partner (or co-parent/support team) together right now?
* Are there family rituals (with grandparents, aunts/uncles, friends) that help strengthen your child's community and model healthy connections?
* How do you prioritize conversations about your emotional needs, and who do you trust to talk with besides your partner?
* What's one thing you wish more people understood about this phase of parenting, and how can you start that conversation?

TEENAGERS: **Maintaining Emotional Intimacy While Parenting Teens**

* How do you and your partner stay emotionally connected while navigating the independence of your teen?
* Who outside your immediate family offers emotional support or perspective during this complex stage, and how do you make space to connect with them?

* Are there family dynamics (e.g., with in-laws, siblings, etc.) that need to be reevaluated to maintain your emotional health?
* What shared values help ground your connection with your partner or support system as parenting changes shape?
* What boundaries are important now around emotional labor, and how can you share that with your community?

ADULT CHILDREN: **Reflecting on Connection and Growth as Partners and Parents**

* Looking back, what small habits helped maintain emotional closeness through all stages of parenting?
* How has your relationship with extended family or your broader community impacted your emotional well-being as a parent?
* What parts of your emotional journey, especially moments of self-compassion, do you feel proud to model for your adult children?
* How have friendships or chosen family played a role in sustaining your connection and resilience through the years?
* What kind of emotional connection do you still want to foster with your partner, adult children, or community?

Rediscovering Your Sexual Self

After your baby is born, everything starts to change: how you see yourself, how you see your partner, even the names you call each other. Maybe your partner starts calling you "Mama" or "Mom," and while it comes from a loving place, it lands differently. You might feel proud of the name and what it represents, but also uncomfortable, like it doesn't fully belong to you yet. It can feel like you've stepped into a role you haven't completely grown into, while still trying to hold onto who you were before. You might notice small moments that bring that feeling into sharper focus. Maybe when your partner calls you "Mom," it makes you pause, like a reminder that life has shifted in a way that can't be undone. Maybe you crave hearing your own name or a familiar pet name again, something that reminds you of the person you still are underneath the diapers, feeding schedules, and constant giving. It can feel discombobulating when the version of you who once existed as a partner, friend, or lover has been replaced by "Mom." Somewhere in the blur of those early months, it can start to feel like you and your partner have gone from being "us" to being a team that's always managing, planning, and troubleshooting. The dynamic changes, and that easy closeness you once shared can start to fade.

It's normal to miss the version of yourself who didn't have to think about sleep schedules or burp cloths before leaning in for a kiss. It's normal to wonder how to move between nurturing your baby and wanting to feel desired again.

That in-between space, the gap between the caregiver and the partner, can feel uncomfortable and confusing. For some, like me, the shift from partners to co-parents became a permanent one. But even now, I can look back and see how that transition held important truths about love and identity. Motherhood didn't erase the person I was before, it asked me to integrate her into the person I was becoming. It's messy and nonlinear, but it's part of the growth that comes with building (or rebuilding) a sense of self after baby. So if you find yourself struggling with that shift, missing who you were, missing how things used to feel, know that it's part of the story. You can still honor your role as a parent while staying connected to the parts of you that existed long before the word "Mom." Those parts are still there, waiting to be seen, named, and brought back into the light in your own time.

Resources: *Mating in Captivity* by Esther Perel and *Sex Talks* by Vanessa Marin provide insightful approaches to rekindling intimacy and connection post-baby. Perel encourages parents to redefine intimacy by exploring how desire can thrive amid the demands of parenting, while Marin emphasizes the importance of open, honest conversations around needs and boundaries to deepen connection. Together, these resources offer practical and compassionate strategies to help couples rediscover their romantic bond, bridging the gap between their roles as parents and partners.

PRE-CHILD PLANNING: **Setting Intentions for Balancing Partnership and Parenthood**

* How did the relationships you observed growing up (your parents or caregivers) influence your ideas about partnership and intimacy during parenthood?
* What do you hope your connection will look like after becoming parents, and what are you afraid it might look like?
* In what ways can your close friends or community support you in maintaining the relationship with your partner, even with the changes a baby brings?
* What language or gestures help you feel seen as a partner, not just a future parent?

DURING PREGNANCY: **Preparing for Role Transitions and Connection**

✱ How has your relationship shifted since becoming pregnant or preparing for a baby together?

✱ How do you want to stay connected to your sense of identity, sexuality, and partnership as your body or roles change?

✱ What kinds of conversations can you have now with extended family or chosen family about giving you space to grow into your new roles without pressure or judgment?

✱ How can you begin naming and exploring the tension between your future parenting identity and your individual self?

POSTPARTUM: **Reclaiming Identity and Connection Beyond the Role of Parent**

✱ How does it feel to be seen primarily as a "parent," and what part of you still wants to be recognized as something more?

✱ When was the last time you felt connected to yourself, not just as a caregiver, but as a person with your desires, preferences, or needs?

✱ What types of connection (emotional, physical, sexual, or social) feel safe, nurturing, or overwhelming right now?

✱ In what ways are you grieving or missing the "you" from before parenthood, and how would you like to reintroduce that version of yourself?

✱ How can your village (friends, family, or caregivers) support you in carving out space for your relationship, without adding pressure or guilt?

- What do you need from your partner or support network to feel more in touch with your emotional or sexual self?

TODDLER YEARS: **Balancing Parenting Demands with Relationship Needs**

- How do you feel about your identity as a partner and individual today, and how has that changed since becoming a parent?
- What messages are you receiving from your community, culture, or family about what intimacy "should" look like right now?
- How can you talk with your partner, or even a close friend, about what you miss or crave in your relationship without guilt or shame?
- What role does playfulness or curiosity play in helping you reconnect with your sexual self?

4–8 YEARS: **Strengthening Your Relationship as Your Family Grows**

- How have you and your partner changed as individuals, and how can you make space to fall in love with the people you've each become?
- What does connection look like beyond sex? How do you express desire, admiration, or affection for each other now?
- Are there ways your community or extended family could support more couple time or deeper adult friendships?
- What kinds of role models do you want to be for your kids when it comes to relationships and intimacy?

9–12 YEARS: **Modeling a Loving Partnership for Your Preteen**

- How do you and your partner balance parenting and intimacy in a way that's visible (and healthy) for your kids to witness?
- What old patterns are you ready to let go of, about roles, responsibility, or connection, and what new ones do you want to try?
- How are you opening up conversations with peers or siblings about the evolving nature of long-term relationships and staying connected?
- What does it mean for you to feel desired, respected, or emotionally close at this stage?

TEENAGERS: **Prioritizing Connection During Busy Teen Years**

- What do your teenagers notice or ask about your relationship, and how do you want to respond in a way that reflects your values?
- How do you and your partner (or co-parent) reconnect when life is busy, and what's getting in the way of that right now?
- Are there ways that your chosen family or community supports your relationship or creates space for your needs as a couple?
- What does it mean to evolve as partners in this chapter, and how do you check in with each other about whether you're still aligned?

ADULT CHILDREN: **Reflecting on Connection and Growth as a Couple**

- What reflections do you and your partner have about how your relationship survived or shifted during the parenting years?

* How do you talk with your adult children about what a genuine, evolving partnership looks like, including the messy, beautiful parts?
* What community or social supports help you stay connected now that parenting is no longer your central shared role?
* In what ways do you still seek out pleasure, intimacy, and connection as individuals and as partners, and how do you share that wisdom?

Chapter 7

RETHINKING FOOD AND PARENTING

Food and mealtimes hold a unique place in family life. They can be moments of connection and joy, and they can also bring stress and challenges, especially when it comes to nurturing children's eating habits. Rethinking food and parenting invites us to approach mealtimes differently, focusing on fostering a positive, balanced relationship with food rather than controlling every bite. It involves creating a space where kids can listen to their hunger cues, explore new foods, and feel respected in their choices while parents find peace and confidence in their approach.

The Psychology of Food and Family Dynamics

Psychologically, food is intertwined with emotion, connection, and identity. Research shows that children thrive when mealtimes are calm and supportive, encouraging autonomy and curiosity rather than control. Developing a positive relationship with food starts with trust: trusting children to honor their natural hunger and fullness cues and allowing them to explore food in their own way.

Studies also highlight that children who feel pressured at mealtimes, whether through "just one more bite" or "clean your plate" expectations, are more likely to develop anxiety or rigidity around food. On the other hand, when parents model intuitive eating, encourage exploration, and bring positive energy to the table, children learn to view food as a source of nourishment, not stress. For parents, this approach often requires letting go of control and focusing instead on fostering connection, adaptability, and trust.

Why a Peaceful Approach to Food Matters

When food is approached with flexibility and respect, it creates an environment where children can develop confidence and curiosity about eating. Instead of turning meals into power struggles or sources of frustration, this approach transforms the table into a place of connection, exploration, and joy. By focusing on shared experiences and making food choices a collaborative process, families can establish habits that support both physical and emotional well-being.

In this chapter, we'll explore how to cultivate a positive mealtime atmosphere, honor individual preferences, and navigate cultural and family traditions. My hope is that these strategies will inspire a renewed sense of purpose and connection in your family's approach to food, empowering everyone at the table to feel respected and nourished.

Redefining Mealtime Connection Across the Years

Mealtimes have this uncanny way of turning into battles, especially when you've put thought and effort into cooking something you're sure your child will love, only to be met with a look of disdain or a simple, "No, I don't like it." I remember one evening vividly, I'd made mini homemade pizzas, complete with my son's favorite toppings. I could already picture us sitting down, laughing, and sharing a meal. Instead, he glanced at his plate, pushed it away, and firmly declared, "I don't eat dinner; I all done." In that moment, I felt a wave of frustration mixed with disappointment, and if I'm being honest, a touch of hurt. It stung more than I wanted to admit. I'd spent all afternoon making something I thought would feel special. Part of me wanted him to enjoy the meal, but on a deeper level, I was hoping for some silent affirmation that I was getting this parenting thing right, that my effort was somehow "paying off." After several dinners like this, I began to understand that his reaction wasn't really about the food itself. It was probably his way of asserting some control, or maybe not even being hungry at all, since he spends most of the day snacking anyway, showing me that he was his own little person with preferences and opinions. It didn't stop me from getting annoyed in the moment, but slowly I started to realize the rejection wasn't personal, even if it felt that way.

Growing up, food was never just food. It carried meaning, tradition, and sometimes, unspoken rules. In Slovak culture, there was always this encouragement, sometimes even pressure, to take more or to finish every bite on your plate. I understand now that this likely came from a place of respect, but mostly, survival. Generations before us didn't always know when their next meal would come, so eating everything available was both practical and necessary. That mindset, though born out of scarcity, was passed down through families like mine. While I can appreciate why my parents would insist on clean plates, we live in a different reality today. We're fortunate and privileged enough to have consistent access to food and can approach mealtimes with more flexibility. This became especially clear as I watched my own kids grow. There are weeks when they eat everything in sight, and other times when their appetites seem to vanish, simply because their bodies don't need as much and they survive off of water and a single cheerio. My ex-husband and I used to get so stressed, even frustrated with each other, wondering how to "get them" to eat: Do we offer rewards like an M&M for every bite? Do we push harder? Eventually, we decided to step back and let them guide us. Even if we served what felt like the "right" portion, we started respecting their signals when they said they were done. Once we focused on offering balanced snacks throughout the day and saw that they were still healthy, growing, and hitting milestones, it felt like a huge weight lifted.

And as I thought more about my reactions to the kids not finishing their meals, I realized that my desire for them to enjoy my home-cooked meals wasn't just about nutrition or their hunger; it was about me being validated. The more I reflected, the more I saw how much of my energy was wrapped up in seeking these small, silent nods of approval. It wasn't really fair to any of us. I began to see mealtime as an opportunity not to control or impress, but to connect. With that shift in perspective, I started offering them small choices, nothing major, but enough to let them feel involved, like deciding between carrots or broccoli, or picking their favorite "safe food" to have alongside the new things. It didn't magically end the refusals, but it gave me a script for when I felt powerless: "Okay, then would you like X or Y?" instead of spiraling into frustration. We also began to honor and respect when they would say they're all done, instead of trying to force them to eat more. It's funny how these tiny decisions helped me understand their need for autonomy in a world where so much is decided for them. And slowly, mealtimes became less about what they were eating and more about enjoying the time together, however imperfect it might look. Some nights are still tense, the broccoli gets thrown, or everyone ends up eating toast, but we're not spiraling like we used to. A "successful" meal for me now isn't about a clean plate; it's about sitting together, talking, connecting about our day, and being silly together.

Resource: *Child of Mine* by Ellyn Satter provides insightful guidance on fostering a positive mealtime experience, focusing on honoring a child's autonomy and natural cues. This approach emphasizes letting go of the need to control each bite, encouraging parents to enjoy meals as a shared experience rather than a test of their child's willingness to comply.

PRE-CHILD PLANNING: **Setting the Tone for Future Mealtimes**

* What kind of mealtime dynamics did you and your partner/co-parent grow up with, and how did those shape your beliefs about food and connection?
* How did adults in your lives respond to picky eating or food refusal, and what messages did you internalize?
* What emotions come up when someone doesn't enjoy a meal you prepared?
* What does an ideal mealtime feel like to you in mood and connection?
* How can you begin conversations with close family or community about their role in future meals (e.g., babysitting, holiday hosting)?

DURING PREGNANCY: **Exploring Food Values and Emotional Ties**

* What values around food, like nourishment, culture, routine, or flexibility, do you want to carry forward or leave behind?
* What expectations might you unconsciously have about how your child should eat or behave at the table?
* How do you or your partner imagine sharing meals with your child, and where might you differ?
* How can you talk to extended family (e.g., grandparents, close friends) about being supportive during mealtimes without pressure or judgment?
* What emotional needs might mealtimes bring up for you, especially when you're tired or craving validation?

POSTPARTUM: **Building Connection Through Early Feeding**

* How can you turn early meals into playful, low-pressure experiences of exploration and learning, for your baby and yourself?
* What are you telling yourself when your baby refuses, loves, or ignores a food, and where do those interpretations come from?
* How can you and your partner support each other when feedings feel discouraging, messy, or emotionally charged?
* What helps you stay grounded when things don't go "as planned," like throwing food, skipping meals, or shifting preferences?
* How can you involve grandparents or other caregivers in feeding in a way that respects your baby's pace and your parenting choices?

* Are you creating a mealtime environment where curiosity and connection matter more than performance or pressure?

TODDLER YEARS: **Navigating "No" with Respect**

* How do you and your partner stay on the same page when your toddler starts refusing foods they once loved?
* What helps you remain calm when meals turn chaotic?
* How can you include extended caregivers (like daycare staff or grandparents) in respecting your toddler's boundaries without reinforcing picky habits?
* Are you giving your toddler enough say in what's on their plate without turning it into a power struggle?
* How can you show up for each other when meals feel more draining than delightful?

4–8 YEARS: **Finding Rhythm and Routine**

* How can you start involving our child in food prep or grocery shopping to build interest and ownership?
* What do you and your partner/co-parent believe about "good manners" or "cleaning your plate," and where might those beliefs clash?
* How can you model a healthy attitude toward food even when you're stressed or rushed?
* Are you involving grandparents or family in mealtimes in a way that supports your routine?
* What helps you notice and respond to early signs of food anxiety?

9–12 YEARS: **Conversations Around the Table**

* How do you keep mealtimes a space for connection when your preteen is more independent?
* Are you teaching nutrition and balance in a way that invites curiosity rather than guilt?
* How do you hold space for cultural, emotional, or sensory food preferences without judgment?
* Which shared meals with extended family are adding joy, and which might need more boundaries?
* How can you use mealtime as a moment to connect with each other, not just get through the day?

TEENAGERS: **Evolving Traditions**

* How do you maintain connection when meals become irregular or independent?
* Are there any food-based rituals, like taco night or Sunday pancakes, that are still meaningful to keep?
* What helps you navigate food choices without slipping into criticism or control?
* How do you talk about health or nutrition in ways that protect mental well-being?
* Are you honoring the ways teens may want to contribute to family meals, or opt out?

ADULT CHILDREN: **Honoring What Mealtimes Built**

* What role did shared meals play in shaping your family culture?
* Are there recipes, traditions, or routines you want to pass on or revisit?

* How do you now define connection through food with adult children, in-laws, or grandchildren?
* What have you learned about feeding others that you wish you'd known earlier?
* How can you continue building meaningful mealtime rituals with adult kids, especially during holidays or transitions?

Balancing Parental Food Preferences and Children's Needs

Our own eating habits inevitably shape what we serve our kids, but I found that my routines had started to limit the variety my son was exposed to at mealtime. With ADHD, I have a tendency to hyperfocus on specific things, including food, which can be both helpful and limiting. I'd find a few reliable recipes, ones that were easy and guaranteed to be hits, and I'd stick to them, buying the same ingredients each week, making the same meals on repeat. It worked: chicken, hot dogs, pasta, repeat. I could make it on autopilot without stressing, and honestly, that felt like survival some nights. It felt efficient and predictable, which was comforting, especially during busy times when dinner felt like a box to check off, or when I was in a food fixation. (A food fixation with ADHD is when your brain latches onto a particular meal or ingredient and wants it over and over again. It's comforting, familiar, and simplifies decision-making, even if it means variety goes out the window for a while.) But eventually, I noticed that while this worked well for me, my children's diet was becoming a bit… monotonous. They began pushing away anything that wasn't part of their familiar rotation, narrowing their preferences even more. One night I served salmon, feeling proud of myself for cooking something new, and both kids pushed it away without a single bite. I wanted to scream, "But I tried!" My routine, which was supposed to simplify things, had started to close off their willingness to try new foods. I'd unknowingly created a food bubble, one that wasn't doing them any favors in terms of variety or openness to new flavors. Realizing this, I decided to slowly shake things up. Instead of buying the same ingredients every week, I started picking up one or two new items to add a small twist to our usual meals. Maybe I'd swap carrots for yams or try adding a new seasoning to our go-to chicken dish. Each time, I gave them the choice to try it, making it clear that it was entirely up to them. Sometimes they'd take a curious bite, and other times they'd just inspect the food and pass. Sometimes I'd feel that sting of rejection again, but reminding myself that "exposure counts" kept me from giving up.

Over time, I saw a shift. Just as I was pushing myself out of my "safe" food zone, they were starting to open up to new tastes and textures. They became more comfortable at least trying new things, mirroring the small steps I was taking in our kitchen routines. It wasn't a drastic change, no overhauls, no forceful "have another bite then you'll get M&Ms!" Just gradual, gentle nudges that helped us all expand our comfort zones. This experience taught me that flexibility in the kitchen, even in small ways, can be incredibly meaningful. By stepping out of my comfort zone, I encouraged them to step out of theirs. It became a small journey of exploration for us all, showing that sometimes, tiny adjustments in our routines can open the door to bigger growth in the long run.

Resource: *The Family Dinner* by Laurie David is a helpful guide for parents wanting to bring variety and joy into family meals. It emphasizes making mealtimes a space for connection and offers practical tips for encouraging kids to try new foods while respecting their tastes.

For families, it's a supportive resource that promotes a relaxed, inclusive environment around food.

PRE-CHILD PLANNING: **Knowing Ourselves and Each Other**

* What kinds of food preferences or routines do you and your partner/co-parent rely on for comfort, and how might those shape what you serve your child?
* How did your parents respond to "picky eating," and what beliefs did that create in you?
* Are there sensory or emotional needs (like predictability or control) that come into play with how you approach meals?
* How might your neurodiversity, mental health, or cultural identity affect your food habits, and how can you talk about that with compassion?
* What kind of flexibility do you want to start building now to prepare for your child with different needs or preferences?

DURING PREGNANCY: **Laying a Flexible Foundation**

* How do you and your partner react when a familiar food routine is disrupted?
* Are you making space for one another's comfort foods while staying open to exploring new ones?
* What language are you using around food (e.g., "good," "bad," "healthy," "junk") and how might you want to shift that?
* What messages about food variety or "clean eating" do you hope to model or unlearn?

* How can you discuss with family or community now the importance of respecting your future child's food preferences and needs?

POSTPARTUM: **Creating a Flexible, Curious Approach to Feeding**

* How do you notice and respond (emotionally and physically) when your baby accepts or rejects a food, and what might that reflect in you?
* Are you making room for small moments of curiosity and play, rather than focusing on how much is eaten?
* How are you and your co-parent dividing or sharing feeding responsibilities (like planning, cooking, or cleanup), and does that setup feel balanced or worth revisiting?
* How do you each model openness around food, like trying new things, keeping meals lighthearted, and showing flexibility, even when it's messy or repetitive?
* How can you communicate or support one another if one of you tends toward rigidity, repetition, or food-related stress, so your child experiences a healthy, consistent relationship with food across your routines (or homes)?
* How are you involving extended family or caregivers in feeding in ways that support your baby's exploration and your values?

TODDLER YEARS: **Respecting Repetition Without Getting Stuck**

* What helps you stay grounded when your toddler demands the same food every day?
* How can you introduce something new without turning it into a battle or a bribe?

- Are you noticing any of your habits of rigidity showing up during mealtimes?
- How do you or your partner respond to food waste or rejection?
- What language can you use with extended family (like grandparents) to support variety?

4–8 YEARS: **Teaching Food Flexibility**

- Are you involving your child in shopping, prepping, or tasting in a way that feels fun, not forced?
- How do you help your child express their likes and dislikes, and how do you respond when they do?
- Are you projecting your preferences onto them, or making room for their individuality?
- What helps you model adventurous eating, even when you're tired or not in the mood?
- How can you support teachers, caregivers, or friends in reinforcing your child's agency with food?

9–12 YEARS: **Bridging Independence and Guidance**

- How can you invite your child to take on more responsibility in the kitchen while still guiding gently?
- Are you talking about nutrition and balance in ways that support autonomy rather than control?
- What helps you stay curious rather than reactive when your child dislikes or rejects something you value?

- How are you including culture, heritage, or family traditions in your shared meals without forcing them?
- What meals or snacks can you make together that reflect all your preferences?

TEENAGERS: **Embracing Divergence**

- How are you adjusting when your teen's food choices diverge from yours or become more independent?
- Are you avoiding judgment or commentary that might shut down connection?
- How can you show interest in their evolving tastes without trying to steer them?
- What traditions or rituals still feel worth keeping, and which ones can you let go of or adapt?
- How do you handle family meals when they're less frequent or more on-the-go?

ADULT CHILDREN: **Reflecting on Shared and Divergent Paths**

- How have your food routines changed alongside your child's growing independence?
- What past food patterns or stories do you look back on with pride, regret, or humor?
- What family recipes or rituals do you want to preserve and pass on?
- How can you make room for adult children's new food values, whether they align with yours or not?
- In what ways can shared meals continue to be a place for connection, even if they look different from before?

Honoring Cultural and Family Food Traditions

Food has always been a big part of how I feel connected to home. In Slovak culture, it's common to start every meal with soup, not just on holidays or weekends, but as a daily ritual. Growing up, my mom cooked a different soup and a second course every other day. There was a kind of rhythm to it: lentil soup on Monday, chicken noodle or garlic soup the next, followed by a meat dish or rice and vegetables. My mom cooked in a way that was practical, reliable, healthy, and predictable. This was how she expressed care, and it made our home feel structured, even when life wasn't.

When I had kids, I really wanted to continue that rhythm. I imagined myself making soup from scratch and serving it before every dinner, just like my mom did. I wanted my kids to grow up with the same kind of comfort and cultural grounding, something warm to return to at the end of the day. But I quickly ran into the reality of what my own life looked like. My former husband and I were parenting two small kids, working, managing a household, and navigating our own ADHD, which often made executive functioning tasks like meal planning and prep feel like too much. I'd stand in the grocery store with the recipe pulled up on my phone, only to get overwhelmed, forget half the ingredients, or abandon the plan altogether. Some weeks the veggies for soup would rot in the fridge while we ordered takeout. What felt so natural in my childhood home started to feel impossible in mine.

At first, I felt ashamed of that, like I was letting go of something sacred. I wanted to hold onto my cultural identity, to pass on something meaningful, but the routines I was trying to replicate just didn't work for the kind of support I needed. I was holding myself to a standard that didn't take into account the life I was actually living. So, I started to let go of the idea that honoring tradition meant doing things exactly the way they were done before. I now use meal delivery services most weeks. I create a loose food plan that leaves room for flexibility and last-minute changes. When I have the time and energy, I'll still make Slovak soups, especially around the holidays, when it feels grounding and nostalgic, but I no longer see it as something I have to do in order to be "doing it right." I'm honoring where I come from, while also honoring my limits, and I recognize that even having the option to outsource meals, to pick and choose what traditions I continue, comes with privilege that my family growing up didn't have, and many parents don't. Going forward, I'm not trying to completely reenact my past, but instead accept myself for where I'm at and give myself permission to be different from what I was brought up with. My kids may not grow up with soup every night, but I hope they'll still feel what I felt: warmth, care, and the sense that food can be a form of love, even if it comes from a takeout container some nights.

Resource: In *The Cooking Gene*, Michael W. Twitty illuminates how culinary traditions shape identity, memory, and belonging across generations. By weaving together personal narratives, ancestral recipes, and deep-rooted historical research, the book invites readers to explore how food connects us to our heritage while honoring evolving tastes. It encourages families to bring cultural rituals into their kitchens, not by replicating history perfectly, but by adapting old recipes in a way that welcomes everyone at the table. For parents, it's a moving and practical guide to blending ancestral traditions with personal preference, helping families define their heritage through food in a living, dynamic way.

PRE-CHILD PLANNING: **Exploring Food Heritage and Identity**

* What food traditions did you and your partner/co-parent grow up with, and how did they shape your sense of family or belonging?
* Are there any holiday meals, rituals, or dishes you want to keep, modify, or leave behind?
* How do your cultural or religious identities influence how you feel about meals, hospitality, or food sharing?
* Have you noticed any tensions between your food traditions, whether in ingredients, expectations, or roles in the kitchen?
* What kind of shared traditions can you imagine creating with your future child, chosen family, or community?

DURING PREGNANCY: **Making Room for Old and New**

* Are you starting to talk about which cultural dishes or practices you want to introduce to your child early on?
* How do you want to blend or navigate the differences in your families' traditions?
* Are there any stereotypes or assumptions about food from your own or each other's cultures you want to be mindful of?
* What kind of mealtime or food rituals do you hope to create for seasonal celebrations or milestones?
* How might you include extended family in cultural food traditions while still setting your tone as new parents?

POSTPARTUM: **Sharing Culture and Legacy Through Early Food**

* What cultural or family foods feel meaningful to introduce, even if it's just for taste, smell, or exposure?
* Are there familiar dishes, spices, or smells from your upbringing that you're starting to bring into your baby's world?
* How are you involving grandparents or relatives in passing down food traditions, through stories, meals, or shared rituals?
* How do you gently hold and communicate your values around feeding when other family members have strong opinions or expectations?
* Are you giving yourselves grace if your child doesn't immediately enjoy the foods you hoped they would love?
* What helps you balance honoring tradition with the realities of postpartum life and modern parenting?

TODDLER YEARS: **Blending Fun with Familiarity**

* How can you include your toddler in meal prep, rituals, or food-related celebrations in playful ways?
* What traditional meals can you simplify or adapt for toddler hands and tastes?
* How do you respond when your child resists or refuses foods that hold cultural or sentimental value?
* Are you helping them form emotional connections to food through stories, songs, or smells?

4–8 YEARS: **Building Memories and Meaning**

* Which food traditions are becoming part of your family rhythm, and how are you explaining them?
* How can you involve your child in selecting or preparing meals for holidays or birthdays?
* Are you telling stories from your own childhood meals to build intergenerational connection?
* What helps you stay flexible if a tradition needs to evolve or be skipped some years?
* How do you invite curiosity about other cultures' food traditions while honoring your own?

9–12 YEARS: **Deepening Understanding of Identity**

* Are you teaching your child how to prepare family recipes or understand why certain foods matter culturally?
* What questions are they asking about their heritage, and how are you responding?
* How do you talk about cultural foods at school, with friends, or in public spaces, especially if they differ from the norm?
* Are you checking in on whether your traditions still feel meaningful or if they need adjusting?

TEENAGERS: **Ownership and Expression**

* How are you responding if your teen doesn't want to participate in a tradition, or wants to adapt it?
* What food traditions still feel important to them? Are you asking?

* How are you inviting them to cook, share, or even create new rituals around food and identity?
* How do you maintain cultural connection while making room for their unique values and beliefs?

ADULT CHILDREN: **Reflecting On What Food Meant**

* What memories stand out when you think of meals from their childhood?
* Are there dishes, practices, or symbols they want to carry into their own homes or families?
* How do you stay connected through food, whether around a table or across distance?
* What old traditions have evolved, and what new ones have you built together as adults?
* How can you continue to use food as a way to gather, celebrate, and stay close, even as roles shift?

Chapter 8

RAISING SOCIAL JUSTICE–MINDED CHILDREN: BUILDING COMPASSION, CURIOSITY, AND COURAGE

In today's interconnected world, raising children with social awareness is more essential than ever. Social justice parenting is about fostering compassion, curiosity, and courage, helping kids grow into empathetic, self-aware individuals who value diversity and fairness. This approach extends beyond singular lessons; it's woven into the everyday interactions and conversations that help children build emotional intelligence, respect for differences, and the confidence to advocate for what's right.

The Psychology of Social Awareness and Empathy

Psychologically, children begin forming ideas about fairness and difference at an early age. Research shows that by preschool, children notice disparities in how people are treated and can start to develop empathy and moral reasoning. Parents play a critical role in nurturing this awareness by creating an environment that values inclusion and encourages open conversations about diversity and fairness.

Teaching children about social justice also builds "moral courage," the ability to stand up for fairness even when it's uncomfortable. Studies suggest that children who learn to recognize bias and unfairness are more likely to engage in prosocial behaviors, such as showing kindness, building inclusive communities, and advocating for others. These skills set the foundation for lifelong empathy and action, preparing children to navigate a diverse world with integrity and respect.

Why Raising Social Justice–Aware Kids Matters

Equipping children with the tools to navigate social justice issues empowers them to understand and engage with the complexities of the world around them. By teaching empathy, critical thinking, and respect for diversity, parents give children a framework to embrace differences and actively challenge prejudice. These lessons go beyond individual actions; they inspire children to contribute positively to their communities, build bridges across differences, and foster a sense of purpose in creating a more equitable world.

In this chapter, we'll explore ways to integrate social justice values into your parenting journey. From reflecting on privilege to building cultural awareness and teaching empathy, this chapter offers tools to help your child approach differences with kindness, engage with the world thoughtfully, and stand up for fairness when it matters most.

Reflecting on Privilege and Isms

Helping our kids make sense of fairness, power, and empathy can start with how we examine our own choices, especially the ones that cause discomfort or make us pause. For me, one of those moments came after my ex-husband and I decided to start hiring professional cleaners every few months. On the surface, it felt like a smart move. Living with ADHD, both of us can struggle with executive functioning, and staying on top of deep cleaning while juggling parenting and work felt like too much. But as soon as we made the decision, I noticed this tightness in my chest. I felt grateful, yes, but also conflicted, like I was betraying something I'd grown up believing in.

In my childhood home, hiring help to clean was never even an option. Financially, it just wasn't something we could afford, but even beyond that, I was taught that cleaning your own home was a matter of pride. Every Sunday, we'd scrub, vacuum, and wipe down every corner together as a family. It was exhausting, but it meant something, and we did it together. It was how we took care of ourselves and showed respect for our home. So, when my ex-husband first suggested getting help, my knee-jerk reaction was guilt, like I should be able to handle this on my own, or that I was taking a shortcut I hadn't earned. I remember even saying, "We can do it ourselves, if you don't want to, I can!" when deep down I knew I didn't actually have the capacity. His experience was different; he grew up with house cleaners, and for him, this was a neutral, even routine decision. It wasn't emotionally loaded. That contrast made me stop and reflect on our different upbringings and how deeply my internal stories about work, class, and "deserving" support were shaped by the systems I grew up in.

And if I'm being honest, part of what I needed to confront was my privilege. I live in British Columbia, and I'm a white, cisgender, heterosexual woman in a dual-income household. While I came to Canada as an immigrant, I also benefit from immense structural privilege. I've had access to education, health care, and professional opportunities that aren't distributed equally. The fact that I *can* outsource domestic labor now is a direct result of those layered advantages. So yes, I had to untangle what this meant for me, but I also had to sit with what it meant systemically. It hit me one day when our cleaner arrived with her own supplies, smiling and kind as always, while I was rushing out the door with a matcha latte in hand. The imbalance was right there in front of me. I have come to recognize that while this support eases a burden for me, the person providing it may not have had the same set of choices I've had. And I've also worked on noticing when the narratives I've absorbed, like "you should be able to do it all yourself," are rooted in a mix of classism, internalized capitalism, and outdated ideas about womanhood and worth.

As a parent, I know my kids are watching not just what I say about fairness and empathy but how I live it. That means staying accountable to my blind spots and being willing to admit when something feels complicated. I'm still learning how to hold the tension between gratitude and discomfort, between receiving help and honoring the people who provide it. These moments aren't always clean or easy, but they offer powerful openings to practice what I hope to teach my kids: Awareness isn't about shame; it's about responsibility. Privilege doesn't have to be something we deny or feel guilty for; it's something we can acknowledge, use with intention, and talk about openly, especially with the people we love. If my kids can grow up seeing that privilege is real, nuanced, and something to be used thoughtfully, then maybe they'll learn to approach their own choices with the same care.

Resource: *Stamped (For Kids)* by Jason Reynolds and Ibram X. Kendi is a wonderful guide for parents and kids to begin exploring race, privilege, and equality in accessible, friendly language. It helps us start those early conversations, fostering an awareness of fairness and inclusion.

PRE-CHILD PLANNING: **How Our Stories Shape Our Lens**

* How were you and your partner taught (explicitly or implicitly) to think about race, class, gender roles, disability, or other differences?
* When did you first realize that your experiences in the world weren't universal?
* How has your access to resources or safety shaped your views on fairness and hard work?
* What privileges do you carry, and how do they affect the kind of parents you might become?
* How do you want to raise a child who sees injustice clearly, but isn't weighed down by shame or defensiveness?

DURING PREGNANCY: **Practicing Awareness**

* What conversations are you having about how systems like racism, sexism, or ableism might shape your child's world?
* Are you thinking about the ways privilege shows up in your birth plan, health-care access, or parenting choices?
* How are you staying open to learning from voices different from your own, especially marginalized ones?
* How do you plan to talk about fairness and injustice with family and friends who may not share your views?

POSTPARTUM: **Planting Seeds of Gratitude, Justice, and Awareness**

* What messages (intentional or not) are you modeling about power, labor, and gratitude in your daily routines?
* How do you talk about and honor the roles of caregivers, service workers, or others whose labor supports your family's well-being?
* Are you creating small rituals, language, or storytime moments that introduce ideas of inclusion, belonging, and mutual care?
* When you access support (childcare, therapy, household help), how do you acknowledge that privilege with honesty and humility?
* What are both you and your partner/co-parent learning about your identities, blind spots, or values now that you're shaping a child's understanding of the world?
* How do you create space to question systems that expect parents to "do it all," and who is most impacted when those expectations go unchallenged?

TODDLER YEARS: **Fairness and Helpers**

* What do you say when your toddler points out differences like skin tone, mobility, clothing, or homes?
* How do you help them understand the concept of fairness when they say, "That's not fair"?
* Are you naming who is often excluded or underrepresented in the spaces you all move through?
* How do you talk about kindness in ways that go beyond being "nice" and move toward equity?
* Are you modeling allyship, such as standing up or speaking out, in age-appropriate ways?

4–8 YEARS: **Big Feelings and Bigger Questions**

✱ How do you help your child explore questions like, "Why don't some people have houses?" or "Why do people get treated unfairly?"

✱ What books, shows, or conversations are giving them tools to notice injustice and ask questions?

✱ How are you talking about consent, gender roles, race, and ability at this stage?

✱ Are you helping them navigate situations where friends or family make exclusionary or biased comments?

✱ How do you involve them in community care, like mutual aid, volunteering, or solidarity?

9–12 YEARS: **Building Language and Advocacy**

✱ How do you support them when they notice and name social injustice, especially when it feels confusing or overwhelming?

✱ What are you doing to unpack the history behind the systems that create inequality, racism, colonialism, classism, etc.?

✱ How do you talk about identity and intersectionality in ways that make room for curiosity and nuance?

✱ Are you encouraging them to ask, "Who's missing from this room, story, or decision?"

✱ How do you check in with them (and yourselves) about the difference between guilt and responsibility?

TEENAGERS: **Power, Identity, and Action**

✱ Are you making room for them to challenge you, and what do you do when that happens?

* How do you talk about privilege in their lives without defensiveness, and make space for their evolving views?
* Are you modeling what it looks like to stay in the discomfort of learning, unlearning, and accountability?
* How are you helping them navigate their own identities, especially if they hold marginalized or mixed experiences?
* In what ways are you encouraging them to move from awareness into action, in their own voice and at their own pace?

ADULT CHILDREN: **Continuing the Work Together**

* How do you reflect as a family on the ways you've benefitted from or been harmed by systems of power?
* What are you proud of in the way you raised awareness around justice, and what might you have done differently?
* How do you support your adult children in using their voice, platform, or resources toward collective care?
* Are you continuing to grow and learn together about equity, reparations, and systemic change?
* How do you create space for generational repair, especially if your values have shifted over time?

Understanding Cultural Diversity

Raising open-hearted, inclusive children means helping them make sense of the beautiful mix of cultures, traditions, and histories around them. Living here in British Columbia, especially in the Greater Vancouver area, we're surrounded by so much cultural richness. Our community is shaped by generations of immigration, by Indigenous stewardship of the land, and by the ways people from all over the world live, work, celebrate, and learn side by side. You don't have to go far to experience this. On any given weekend, you might find us walking through Italian Day on Commercial Drive, catching performances at the Sakura Festival, sampling food at an Indian celebration, or listening to live music at a Filipino street fair. Our kids might not realize it now, but these experiences are shaping their view of what "normal" means, and for us, we hope normal always includes diversity.

I was born in Slovakia, in a town where nearly everyone looked the same and spoke the same language. Whenever I would go back and visit, I wasn't exposed to much cultural or racial diversity, and to be honest, there was a lot of fear and bias in the ways people talked about anyone perceived as "different." In particular, there was a long and painful history of systemic discrimination against the Roma people. Looking back, I can see how those messages shaped my early views, even when they weren't said outright. I absorbed the idea that difference was suspicious, something to be wary of or distanced from. I can still remember the way adults lowered their voices when speaking about Roma families, how quickly I learned that "difference" was something you didn't question but just accepted. It's taken time, self-reflection, and unlearning to recognize how those early narratives showed up in my thinking, and to choose differently as a parent. Sometimes that unlearning is awkward, like catching myself about to use a phrase I heard growing up, or realizing I don't have all the right words when my kids ask a hard question, but I'd rather stumble through it than pass on silence.

That's part of why living here, in a place where diversity is an essential part of daily life, feels like such a gift, and a responsibility. My ex-husband and I talk often about how we want to co-parent our kids to be respectful, curious, and aware. That means celebrating languages they hear that are different from their own, not mocking them. It means noticing and honoring clothing choices like hijabs, turbans, yarmulkes, or regalia, and explaining their meaning with respect and wonder, not discomfort or dismissal. It means helping them understand that people express identity in different ways, including through religion, gender, culture, or ability, and that there's beauty and power in that. It also means acknowledging the Indigenous lands we live on and doing more than just naming them. We read picture books with stories by Indigenous authors and talk about what it means to be guests on this land. Some nights, that's a quick two-minute chat over bedtime stories, and other times it'll be a bigger conversation about history, fairness, or respect. We don't always get it perfect, and I know we'll keep messing up and trying again, but that's part of the point: Our kids see us practicing what it looks like to stay open, humble, and willing to learn.

Resource: *Raising White Kids* by Jennifer Harvey is a helpful guide that encourages parents to cultivate empathy, respect, and curiosity about other cultures and experiences. It provides practical ideas for parents to introduce the concept of diversity, model respect, and approach differences with openness.

PRE-CHILD PLANNING: **Reflecting on How We Were Taught to See Differences**

* What were some of the messages you received about people who looked, dressed, or believed differently from you when you were growing up?
* How did your schools, neighborhoods, or families talk about culture, race, or religion, if at all?

- Have you ever felt discomfort or judgment around certain cultural practices, and what do you think shaped that feeling?
- What are some experiences that helped expand your understanding of cultural diversity as an adult?
- How might your cultural backgrounds shape the way you talk to your kids about inclusion and empathy?

DURING PREGNANCY: **Setting Intentions for an Inclusive Family Culture**

- How do you want your home to reflect the values of curiosity, openness, and respect when it comes to different cultures or identities?
- Are there ways you can start incorporating books, artwork, or music that show a wide range of people, languages, and traditions?
- How can you hold space for your child to ask questions about differences without shaming them for their curiosity?
- What cultural traditions or experiences from your background do you want to share, and how can you also make space for others'?
- How can you gently challenge biases you still carry, even if they're uncomfortable to admit?

POSTPARTUM: **Modeling Respect and Belonging from the Start**

- What kinds of books, songs, or toys are you bringing into your home, and what messages might they be sending about who belongs?
- How do you model warmth, curiosity, and respect when interacting with people from different backgrounds in your community?

* What do you say out loud when your child notices someone expressing cultural or religious identity through clothing or language?
* Are you showing appreciation for the people who support your family, especially those whose labor is often undervalued or overlooked?
* How can you talk openly, as a couple or family, about questions that come up when navigating differences, instead of brushing them aside?
* What are simple ways you can begin to teach respect and inclusion, even before your baby fully understands the words?

TODDLER YEARS: **Building Comfort with Questions About Difference**

* What do you say when your toddler asks something blunt or surprising about someone's appearance, clothing, or accent?
* Are you naming cultural celebrations when you go to festivals or public events, and using them as chances to learn together?
* How do you respond when your child notices that some people are treated differently or left out?
* Are you choosing stories and shows that reflect more than just one cultural lens or type of family?
* How do you help your toddler feel proud of their background while being curious about others?

4–8 YEARS: **Exploring Identity, Fairness, and Celebration**

* When your child brings up something unfair that they've seen or heard, how can you support their sense of justice without overwhelming them?

- Are you helping them understand that people's differences, like skin color, language, religion, or traditions, are part of what makes communities strong?
- How can you talk about privilege in small, accessible ways, like who gets included or excluded in certain spaces or stories?
- What are some ways you can involve your child in cultural events or community projects that honor inclusion?
- Are you asking them what they notice about diversity in their school, books, or media, and what they think about it?
- How do you model curiosity when *you* don't know the answer to a question they ask about someone else's identity?

9–12 YEARS: **Encouraging Perspective-Taking and Advocacy**

- How can you support your child in noticing who's missing from the stories they hear, the history they learn, or the spaces they're in?
- Are you talking openly about stereotypes or biases they're beginning to pick up from school, media, or peers?
- What's helping them feel proud of their roots, and how can you encourage them to learn about the roots of others, too?
- How do you talk as a family about Indigenous history and presence in the place you live?
- Are you giving them opportunities to ask big questions about fairness, inclusion, and what they can do to help?

* How do you, as parents, continue to check your blind spots and share that process with your kids?

TEENAGERS: **Deepening Understanding and Supporting Action**

* How can you support your teen if they want to speak up about injustice at school or in their friend group?
* What are some ways they can learn from people outside of their identity group, through books, conversations, art, or mentorship?
* Are you creating space to talk about their experiences of feeling excluded or different, and what they've noticed in others?
* What media are they engaging with, and how do they feel about who is or isn't represented?
* How are you, as adults, continuing to challenge yourselves and show that this learning is lifelong?

ADULT CHILDREN: **Reflecting on the Impact of Family Values Around Inclusion**

* Looking back, what do you think you got right, and what could you have done better when it comes to talking about race, culture, and equity?
* How do you continue learning from your adult children, especially if they've moved into more diverse circles than we ever had?
* Are there family traditions, stories, or habits that reflect inclusion and cultural awareness that you're proud to pass on?
* What are some of the ways you see your children modeling inclusion or equity in their own families, careers, or communities?

* How can you keep showing up with humility and curiosity, especially when your kids challenge you on outdated beliefs or blind spots?
* What does it mean to you to be part of a community, and how do you honor the many cultures and identities that shape it?

Teaching Children About Bullying and Building Empathy

Bullying is still happening, and not just in the ways we remember from our own childhoods. It's in the school hallways, in the yard during recess, in the group chats, and all over social media, often starting younger than we'd like to believe. I've worked with families on both sides of this; kids who were terrified to go to school because of relentless teasing, and kids who had been called into the office for being the ones to cause harm, and what I've seen again and again is that it's almost never as simple as "mean kid, kind kid." It's more layered than that. Bullying often shows up when a child doesn't have the tools or the emotional support to cope with what's going on in their inner world or their home environment. Sometimes it's kids who aren't being seen or heard at home, who are hurting in quiet ways and then act out that pain by trying to gain control somewhere else. I've sat with kids who sobbed after hurting a peer because they didn't even know why they did it, they just felt so full of anger or sadness they had nowhere else to put. What we sometimes call "lateral violence," hurt being passed from one person to another because it has nowhere else to go, shows up early. And kids pick up on power dynamics much earlier than we think.

When I worked in community health care, I supported parents whose kids were being bullied and others whose kids were the instigators, flagged by teachers or other parents for aggressive or harmful behavior. Having kids in either group was incredibly painful for the families involved, and what was so clear to me through that work was just how much children's behavior is shaped by what they see and feel at home and how adults around them talk about others, how they handle stress, how they apologize or don't, how they speak about differences, and how they respond when they make mistakes. Kids are watching all of it. So much of teaching empathy is in how we live, how we repair after conflict, how we treat the person ringing up our groceries, or how we respond to the neighbor who gets on our nerves. That's what they absorb.

On the flip side, when a child is being bullied, they need to know that they can come to their caregivers and be taken seriously. That they won't be told to just toughen up or that "kids will be kids." They need to know that they'll be protected, advocated for, and heard. I've had parents break down in my office because they wished someone had taken *them* seriously when they were the ones being bullied as kids, and now they're determined to do it differently for their children. But we also need to leave space for the moments when our own child might be the one who has caused harm, because the truth is, it could be any of our kids, and we don't want them to lie about it or hide it out of fear. We want to be the ones they come to when they've messed up, when they feel ashamed or confused, or don't know why they said what they said or did what they did. That doesn't mean excusing the behavior, but it does mean showing them that growth and repair are possible, and that being a good person doesn't mean never messing up; it means learning how to take accountability and doing better.

Ultimately, our kids don't need to be perfect, but they do need to know how to face hard truths about themselves, make things right when they've hurt someone, and stand alongside others when they see harm being done.

And that starts with how we talk, how we listen, how we show up, and how we make home feel like a place where honesty and empathy can actually thrive.

Resource: *The Invisible Boy* by Trudy Ludwig is a beautifully illustrated story that helps children understand how it feels to be left out and the impact of kindness. For parents, it offers a simple, heartfelt way to introduce the concept of inclusion and the difference a little empathy can make.

PRE-CHILD PLANNING: **Reflecting on Our Roots of Empathy and Discipline**

- How was discipline handled in your home growing up, and how did it shape the way you saw authority and kindness?
- Were you ever bullied, or did you witness bullying? How did it affect you long-term?
- Did you ever participate in bullying behavior, and if so, what might have been going on for you at that time?
- How comfortable are you with conflict and repair, and how might that affect how you teach your child about navigating social harm?
- How did your family talk (or not talk) about emotional safety, power, and fairness?
- How can you and your partner create a home where mistakes are part of growth, not something to be punished with shame?

DURING PREGNANCY: **Creating a Culture of Safety and Emotional Honesty**

- How can you model repair after conflict so that your child sees what it looks like to be accountable and kind?

* What kinds of language do you want to use around discipline? Are you focused more on teaching or controlling?
* How can you make space in your parenting to talk openly about feelings, including ones like jealousy, shame, and anger?
* What kinds of friendships do you want your child to witness you cultivating, especially when it comes to kindness and loyalty?
* What are some ways you can begin practicing compassion toward yourself, so your child sees that modeled from the start?
* What will you do if you find out your child has been unkind to someone else? How can you respond with both accountability and love?

POSTPARTUM: **Modeling Emotionally Safe and Compassionate Relationships**

* How do you talk to your baby when they're upset?
* In moments of stress, how do you treat yourself and your partner, and what tone does that set in your home?
* What kinds of books, songs, or everyday interactions are you using to reflect empathy, kindness, and inclusion?
* How do you want to model empathy when talking about others, especially those who are different in ability, background, or identity?
* How can you begin to create a family culture where asking for help, expressing emotions, and being vulnerable are met with safety, not shame?
* Who in your community or family can you trust to model compassion and connection alongside you as your child grows?

TODDLER YEARS: **Learning Big Feelings and Social Boundaries**

- How can you help your toddler name their feelings instead of acting them out through pushing, hitting, or yelling?
- What do you say when they act out or hurt someone? Are you teaching them how to repair, not just punishing them?
- How can you show them that everyone makes mistakes, but you always try to make it right?
- How do you celebrate differences with your toddler? Do you talk about different bodies, clothes, or ways of playing with curiosity and kindness?
- Who are the friends and family members that you can highlight as examples of compassion and emotional strength?

4–8 YEARS: **Practicing Empathy and Learning to Name Harm**

- How would you want someone to respond if your child were the one being left out, and how can you show that to other kids?
- How do you help your child understand that kids who act unkindly often have pain they haven't learned how to name?
- What do you do when your child tells you someone was mean to them? Do you listen, validate, and take it seriously?
- How do you help your child stand up for someone else without putting themselves at risk?
- When your child makes a mistake, how do you talk to them about repair without using shame or blame?

* How can you celebrate being a friend who notices who's left out and makes space for them?

9–12 YEARS: **Exploring Accountability, Power, and Belonging**

* How does your child talk about the social dynamics at school? Do they feel safe, included, or on edge?
* Have you asked them how they would handle it if they saw someone being bullied or left out?
* Do you talk about how power works in friend groups, and how people sometimes try to get power by putting others down?
* Have you made it clear to your child that they can come to you whether they've been hurt or they've hurt someone else?
* What kind of role models (in real life, books, or shows) can you point to when talking about courage and kindness?
* What helps your child feel proud of who they are without needing to prove they're better than someone else?

TEENAGERS: **Owning Values and Choosing Courage**

* What do you believe as a family about stepping in when someone is being hurt?
* How does your teen talk about power, popularity, and peer pressure, and do they feel supported in setting boundaries?
* Have you talked about online bullying and group chats? Do they know how to protect their mental health online?

- ✱ How do you respond when your teen admits to getting something wrong or being part of harmful behavior?
- ✱ How can you model that vulnerability isn't weakness?

ADULT CHILDREN: **Reflecting on the Legacy of Emotional Awareness**

- ✱ What do you remember about how your family handled conflict, and what parts are you proud to carry forward?
- ✱ How do you talk now, as adults, about power and empathy in your relationships, workplaces, or communities?
- ✱ What does "repair" look like in your family? How have you practiced making amends and reconnecting after conflict?
- ✱ How can you keep modeling emotional honesty and kindness in the way you show up for one another today?
- ✱ Are there things you'd like to do differently in your families, partnerships, or communities based on what you've lived and learned?

Chapter 9

TEACHING SAFETY AND CONSENT TO CHILDREN

As parents, we carry a deep instinct to protect our children and help them grow into confident, self-assured individuals who understand their boundaries and advocate for their well-being. Teaching safety and consent to children allows us to prevent possible future harm, empower them with the tools to navigate relationships, respect their bodies, and develop healthy boundaries with others. For many of us, this journey brings up memories of times when our boundaries weren't respected or when we lacked the language to articulate our discomfort. Reflecting on these experiences can help us reshape the narrative for our children, equipping them with the confidence and skills we wish we had.

Safety and consent education is a lifelong conversation that evolves as children grow. From teaching toddlers the names of their body parts to helping preteens navigate peer dynamics or preparing teens for independent social situations, these lessons lay a foundation of trust, communication, and respect. This chapter provides tools for parents to build that foundation, covering topics like building early body awareness, teaching consent and boundaries, and navigating complex care situations such as sleepovers or babysitters.

The Psychology Behind Safety and Consent

Research shows that children who are taught about body boundaries and consent from an early age are more likely to identify unsafe situations and advocate for themselves. Early education on consent helps children develop a strong sense of autonomy and self-respect, empowering them to set and defend their boundaries while respecting those of others.

For parents, teaching consent can also be an opportunity to process and heal past experiences around boundaries and safety. These lessons prepare children to navigate social dynamics and create a home environment where open communication is valued, and children feel comfortable seeking guidance when needed.

Why Teaching Safety and Consent Matters

Safety and consent education equips children with essential life skills: understanding and asserting their boundaries, recognizing when someone else's boundaries are being crossed, and confidently navigating social interactions. These lessons foster resilience, empathy, and self-awareness, helping children grow into respectful, empowered adults.

This chapter provides a developmental approach to teaching safety and consent, offering practical strategies tailored to your child's age and stage. From early conversations about body autonomy to preparing teens for complex social situations, the goal is to help you create an environment where safety, trust, and mutual respect are part of everyday life.

Respecting Body Autonomy and Naming Parts Correctly

One of the most powerful things I've learned as a parent is how much our kids absorb from the way we talk about bodies—theirs, our own, each other's, and the people around us. From the very beginning, we have tried to be very mindful of how we introduce body-related language in our home, even when our kids were too young to say much back. When I started saying the words out loud to our children, even in casual ways—"Let's make sure your vulva is clean" or "I'm washing your penis now"—I noticed how awkward it felt. Using accurate anatomical terms like "penis" and "vulva" has become one of those small, daily ways I try to build a foundation of body respect, even if it didn't come naturally to me at first: "Here's your arm," "Let's dry your tummy," "Now your vulva." No shame, no silliness, just straightforward naming.

As they grow, I also think a lot about how gender, culture, and family values will shape what messages they internalize about their bodies. With my son, I'm already noticing how easy it is for the world to comment on his strength, energy, or how "tough" he is. With my daughter, I know the comments may start to tilt toward beauty, cuteness, or her clothes. Even at this age, I feel the pressure. I catch myself sometimes almost saying "You look so pretty" before stopping and shifting to, "I love how creative you're being." It's like unlearning a script that's been handed down to me. What does it mean to raise a daughter in a world obsessed with thinness, politeness, or comparison? What does it mean to raise a son who's allowed to be gentle, emotional, and in tune with his body without shame?

We also need to talk a lot about *all* bodies—bodies that are bigger, smaller, older, disabled, gender diverse—and the way society responds to them. Even though those conversations will become more complex over time, I want the groundwork to be there: Nobody is more worthy of respect than another, differences are normal, beauty isn't something we earn by fitting a standard, and our value isn't tied to how we look or move through the world. This isn't always easy in practice. Sometimes I'll glance in the mirror and mutter something critical about myself without thinking, only to realize little ears are listening. Those moments are a reminder that I'm teaching with my actions as much as my words. Our kids aren't growing up in a bubble; they're absorbing the same noisy, conflicting messages we all did, just sooner and louder, thanks to screens and peers. If our home can be a place where they see bodies spoken about with respect and acceptance, where they feel safe and confident in their own, that's a start I can be proud of, even if I stumble along the way.

Resource: *It's Not the Stork!* by Robie H. Harris is a wonderful book for teaching children the correct anatomical names and understanding their bodies. It uses clear, age-appropriate language that helps normalize these terms in a respectful way.

PRE-CHILD PLANNING: **Exploring How We Learned About Bodies**

* How did your family talk about bodies when you were growing up? What was named and what was left unspoken?
* What words about anatomy feel natural to you now, and which still feel awkward or off-limits?
* How do you think your cultural or religious background shaped the way you think about nudity, modesty, or body image?

* What hopes do you have for how your child will feel in their body, about safety, respect, confidence, or curiosity?
* How do you see your gender (or your partner's) influencing the kind of body-related messages you were raised with?
* What types of body diversity—in size, ability, gender expression—were acknowledged or ignored in your childhood?

DURING PREGNANCY: **Preparing for Body-Aware Parenting**

* When you picture naming your baby's body parts—penis, vulva, chest—how do you feel? Confident? Hesitant? Embarrassed?
* What kinds of comments have you already heard from others about your baby's body, and how do you want to respond to that?
* Are you and your partner aligned on the anatomical terms you will be using with your child? Is there anything you still need to talk through?
* What do you want to model in your tone and language when you talk about your body around your child?
* What types of comments do you feel ready to challenge when it comes to gendered expectations of your baby's appearance?

POSTPARTUM: **Naming the Body from the Start**

* How do you feel about using correct terms like "penis" or "vulva" during diaper changes or bath time? What makes it easier or harder?

- Are there moments you notice yourselves defaulting to nicknames or skipping over naming certain body parts?
- How do you talk about your baby's body around family, and what kinds of language or reactions have you noticed from them?
- How would you respond if a friend or caregiver used a different term than you prefer?
- What values are you trying to model when you name their body parts clearly and without shame?

TODDLER YEARS: **Supporting Body Curiosity**

- What's your reaction when your toddler points to or talks about their body? Do you respond with openness or try to distract?
- How do you talk about body parts in public, and what are you modeling if you seem embarrassed or flustered?
- Have you talked about what to say when your toddler names their penis or vulva in front of others?
- How are you encouraging healthy curiosity while also beginning to introduce concepts like privacy and respect?
- What kinds of messages are your toddler already receiving from extended family or media about appearance or gender?

4–8 YEARS: **Reinforcing Body Respect and Inclusion**

- How are you talking to your child about different types of bodies: big bodies, disabled bodies, gender-diverse bodies?

* What kind of comments do you make about your bodies when you're around them, and what might they be learning from that?
* Do you notice a pattern in how you talk to your son versus your daughter? Are you more likely to praise beauty, strength, or politeness?
* How do you respond when your child comments on someone else's appearance in public? What can you model in that moment?
* How do you talk about clothing, body shape, or food without reinforcing shame or "good" vs. "bad" body messages?

9–12 YEARS: **Naming Changes Without Shame**

* How do you create space for your child to ask about erections, periods, body hair, or breast development without feeling awkward?
* What do you want them to know about body diversity and the way people grow and change, especially if their body doesn't match what they see in the media?
* Have you talked about how society treats boys' and girls' bodies differently and how that might feel confusing or unfair?
* How can you include disability, weight, or gender fluidity in your everyday examples when you talk about people and their bodies?
* How do you respond to their worries or observations about their appearance without brushing them off or jumping to reassurance?

TEENAGERS: **Encouraging Body Confidence and Autonomy**

* How do you check in with your teen about their changing body without making it feel like an interrogation?
* What language are they hearing from peers, social media, or school about what's "normal," and how do you help them make sense of it?
* How do you talk about strength, beauty, health, or hygiene in ways that aren't shaming or rooted in appearance?
* Have you asked them what feels supportive when they're struggling with how they look or feel in their body?
* How do you model body respect in how you talk about yourself and others?

ADULT CHILDREN: **Reflecting on the Legacy of Body Talk**

* When you think back, how did you talk about body parts, privacy, or changes when they were younger, and how do you feel about that now?
* What messages do you hope you passed on about body confidence, respect, or openness?
* How do you keep conversations about health, aging, or physical changes respectful and noninvasive?
* What moments still stand out when you saw them advocate for their body, ask for support, or show confidence?
* How do you want to keep modeling body respect, now as parents of adults, grandparents, or simply as people still growing?

Teaching Consent and Boundaries

Teaching kids about consent and boundaries doesn't have to start with "the talk" when they're teenagers; it can begin in the early years, often through the smallest moments. In our home, it starts with something as simple as giving our children a say in how they greet or say goodbye to people. We offer options: a hug, high-five, fist bump, kiss, or even just a wave. Some days, they run in for a hug; other times, they pull back or just nod, and that's okay. We want them to know their bodies are their own, and they don't owe physical affection to anyone, even to family members. It hasn't always been easy with extended family; I've had to step in a few times and gently say, "They don't feel like hugging right now," and I can feel the awkward silence that follows. But for me, that's part of the work.

This has felt especially important for me, having grown up in Slovakia, where kisses on both cheeks were expected without question. Consent wasn't a concept we discussed; it was assumed you'd comply with social norms, whether you were comfortable or not. I can still remember the times I froze inside but went along with it anyway because saying no didn't feel like an option. So, shifting away from that and teaching our kids that they *can* say no feels both unfamiliar and deeply meaningful. Teaching consent can go beyond physical touch by helping kids understand that they're allowed to have boundaries around their space, their feelings, and their choices. And equally important, they need to learn how to respect others' boundaries too. That means we model it at home: We knock before entering their room, we pause to ask before helping them with something they're doing on their own, and we talk openly when our boundaries are crossed, using language they can understand. Sometimes that means saying things like, "I don't want to be climbed on right now, my body is tired," so they see me as a person with boundaries too.

Consequences are part of this, too, but not in a punitive way. We try to link consequences to the impact of their actions. If a child repeatedly ignores another's "no," we pause play and talk about what happened. If they violate someone's boundary, we focus on repairing and understanding rather than just punishing. It doesn't always look smooth. Sometimes it's a messy five-minute cry before they're ready to talk about it – but those moments stick. We want our kids to grow up knowing that respect, comfort, and choice are not negotiable. And the best way to teach that is by showing it, consistently, patiently, and age-appropriately, as they grow.

Resource: *Let's Talk About Body Boundaries, Consent, and Respect* by Jayneen Sanders provides a helpful guide for teaching consent and body safety to children, offering practical ways to introduce these topics in daily life.

PRE-CHILD PLANNING: **Laying the Foundation for Consent and Respect**

* What did "boundaries" mean in your and your partner's families growing up? Were they spoken or assumed?
* How did people in your childhood homes show or ignore consent, physically or emotionally?
* Are there family or cultural traditions you want to continue? Which ones do you want to reevaluate through the lens of body autonomy?
* How will you support each other if your extended family pushes back on your parenting choices around greetings or affection?
* How can you model asking for consent in our relationships, physically, emotionally, or practically?

DURING PREGNANCY: **Preparing to Model Consent from the Start**

* How do you want to narrate caregiving tasks so they're grounded in respect and clarity, even when your baby is too young to respond?
* What words or tone feel natural to you when talking through actions like diaper changes or bath time?
* Are there family members you need to prepare for your approach to consent and physical affection with your baby?
* How do you check in with each other when boundaries are crossed unintentionally?
* In what ways can you begin modeling consent and emotional boundaries with one another, especially during stressful or exhausting times?

POSTPARTUM: **Practicing Consent and Body Autonomy from the Start**

* How do you or your partner react when your baby resists or squirms during caregiving, and what adjustments can you make to help them feel safer?
* What are simple ways you can offer choice during daily routines (like diaper changes or feeding) to begin teaching bodily autonomy?
* How do you want to support each other in staying consistent with these values, even when things feel chaotic, rushed, or judged by others?
* Are you comfortable gently correcting others if they ignore your baby's cues or boundaries, and how can you explain your choices?
* What does it mean to you to create a home where your child's "no" is respected and their body belongs to them?

TODDLER YEARS: **Encouraging Independence and Respecting "No"**

* How can you encourage your toddler to express preferences without making them feel wrong for saying no?
* How do you explain to extended family or caregivers that you want your toddler to have options for physical affection?
* What stories or books might help reinforce the idea that everyone has the right to their own boundaries?
* How do you repair with your toddler when you cross their boundary out of urgency or frustration?

4–8 YEARS: **Expanding Consent Conversations to Relationships and Play**

* How can you talk with your child about respecting a friend's "no" or body language during play?
* What examples from your friendships could you share to show how boundaries are navigated?
* What do you say when your child asks why someone doesn't want to share, play, or hug?
* How can you model apologies and repair when someone's boundary is crossed?

9–12 YEARS: **Connecting Consent to Growing Independence**

* How can you open up conversations about consent in digital spaces like texting, group chats, or photo sharing?
* Have you shared any (age-appropriate) stories where your boundaries weren't respected? What did you and your kids learn?

* How do you help your child feel confident setting boundaries with friends, teachers, or coaches?
* How can you support them if they feel awkward or worried about disappointing others when they say no?

TEENAGERS: **Reinforcing Consent in Relationships and Digital Life**

* How can you create a safe space for them to talk to you about romantic or social experiences without fear of judgment?
* How can you explain what consent looks like in a dating relationship, or even in a friendship?
* Can you explore with your kids if they've ever felt unsure about how to say no?
* How can you help set and communicate boundaries online, like what you're okay with sharing, seeing, or receiving?

ADULT CHILDREN: **Reflecting on Lifelong Lessons in Consent and Boundaries**

* How can you show respect for your adult child's physical and emotional boundaries?
* How can you model consent and boundary-setting in your own interactions with them?
* How do you repair or reconnect if you accidentally cross a boundary?

Approaching Body Safety, Supervision, and Caregiving Arrangements

With growing awareness of childhood abuse statistics, many parents are reevaluating how they approach conversations about body safety, supervision, and caregiving arrangements. These aren't always easy discussions to have, especially when they push against how we were raised, challenge family norms, or bring up our own experiences. But they're necessary. As a therapist, I've worked with many adults still carrying the weight of childhood abuse, often from people their families trusted: relatives, family friends, coaches, babysitters, etc. This reality has deeply shaped the way I approach body safety with my children and the way I support others in doing the same.

Body safety starts early, far earlier than many of us were taught. And it's not about scaring children; it's about giving them tools, language, and support to understand what's appropriate and what's not. It means teaching them the correct names for body parts, what areas are private, and that they always have the right to say no to unwanted touch, even from adults. It also means helping them understand the difference between a secret and a surprise, and that they can always come to us if something doesn't feel right, even if they're unsure or embarrassed.

But preparing children is only one piece of it. The other part involves navigating these conversations with our partners and families. That might look like having honest, sometimes uncomfortable discussions with a co-parent about your values or fears. It might mean explaining to grandparents why your child isn't expected to hug or kiss anyone goodbye. It might mean setting clear expectations with other parents before a playdate or sleepover: asking who will be home and what kind of supervision will be in place. Some families choose to forgo sleepovers altogether; others create clear "opt-out" plans so children know they can call and leave at any time for any reason.

What's most important is that the message is consistent: "Your body belongs to you. You are allowed to feel safe. You are allowed to speak up. And we will always take you seriously." As children grow, these lessons evolve, from basic rules about private parts and safe touch to more nuanced conversations about boundaries, coercion, and digital safety. These talks don't have to be one big, dramatic sit-down but can be woven into everyday moments: while getting dressed, during bath time, after a confusing situation, or even while watching a show together. What matters is that they're ongoing, and that we, as the adults, are willing to do our own work so we can show up for those conversations with clarity and confidence.

This kind of parenting requires intention, but it also builds deep trust. When kids know they can talk to us without fear or shame, they are better equipped to notice red flags, set boundaries, and ask for help if they need it. And when we involve our partners, families, and wider community in these values, we help create a culture where children's safety and autonomy are truly practiced.

Resource: *The Safe Child Book* by Sherryll Kraizer covers a wide range of scenarios, including how to communicate with your children about safety, sleepovers, and other potentially vulnerable situations, offering strategies for peace of mind.

PRE-CHILD PLANNING: **Laying the Foundation for Safe Care Environments**

* What were the unspoken rules about safety and supervision in your home growing up?
* Are there experiences from your childhood (positive or harmful) that shape how you think about body safety now?
* What boundaries do you feel strongly about, and how can you explain them clearly to a future co-parent or support system?
* How comfortable are you talking about private parts and safe touch using accurate language?

* How can you build a shared approach to sleepovers, babysitters, or time with extended family?
* Who in your community would you trust to care for a future child, and why?

DURING PREGNANCY: **Establishing Guidelines for Future Care Arrangements**

* What do you want to teach your child early on about body safety, and when should those conversations begin?
* How do you feel about letting others care for your baby, even for short periods?
* How do you want to respond if friends or family push back on your boundaries around supervision or physical affection?
* Are there books, courses, or supports you can explore now to build confidence in these topics?
* How can you support your partner if this brings up anxiety or past trauma?
* What values do you want to center on in how you select and train caregivers?

POSTPARTUM: **Creating a Culture of Safety and Trust**

* How can you communicate clearly with family, friends, or recurring caregivers about your expectations for safety, comfort, and respect?
* What helps you notice and respond to your baby's cues of comfort or discomfort, especially with different people or environments?
* Are you feeling any hesitation around letting others hold or care for your baby, and what past experiences or instincts might that be connected to?

* How do you want to introduce body part names or early safety language during routines like diaper changes or bath time?
* What support or language do you need to confidently advocate for your baby's boundaries, especially when well-meaning others dismiss them?

TODDLER YEARS: **Introducing the Concept of Boundaries and Autonomy**

* How can you explain that some body parts are private in a calm, age-appropriate way?
* How does your child respond when you give them choices about physical contact? Are you supporting their "no"?
* Are you and your partner on the same page when it comes to enforcing safety rules, even with family?
* How do you help your child practice saying "stop" or "no" during play?
* What language can you use to reassure your child that they can always come to you if something feels off?

4–8 YEARS: **Encouraging Communication and Independence**

* How does your child react to conversations about body safety? Are they curious, anxious, or disinterested, for example, and how do you adjust your approach?
* Have you practiced scenarios with your child where they can safely say "no" or leave an uncomfortable situation?

* What tools (code word, check-in call) do you use to support safety during sleepovers or playdates?
* Do you model comfort with discussing body autonomy and privacy in everyday life?
* How do you follow up after care situations to create a safe space for sharing?
* What systems do you have in place to support open and honest dialogue?

9–12 YEARS: **Deepening Conversations About Trust and Advocacy**

* Does your child know how to recognize manipulation or pressure, whether from a peer or adult?
* How do you talk about what's appropriate in digital settings (sharing images, group chats, etc.)?
* Have you shared any personal experiences to normalize speaking up and having them trust their instincts?
* How do you respond when your child pushes back on boundaries? Do you stay curious or become dismissive?
* Who are the adults in your child's life that they trust, and how can you help strengthen those relationships?
* Are you talking about the why behind your rules, so they understand it's about safety, not control?

TEENAGERS: **Navigating Complex Care and Social Situations**

* How comfortable does your teen feel talking to you about body autonomy, dating, or safety?
* How do you talk about social situations (parties, dating, time away from home) in a way that feels collaborative instead of controlling?

* What kind of situations might your teen encounter where boundaries get blurry, and how can you prepare for that together?
* What do you want to model in how you talk about and maintain boundaries in your relationships?
* Does your teen know who they can turn to for support beyond you, and how to reach out?
* How do you discuss consent and safety without inducing shame or fear?

ADULT CHILDREN: **Reflecting on Lifelong Lessons in Safety and Boundaries**

* What parts of your early conversations about body safety stuck with your child, and what didn't?
* Have you created space for them to share past experiences, even ones you didn't know about at the time?
* How do you continue to respect their autonomy now, as an adult navigating their own relationships and boundaries?
* What can you learn from their evolving perspectives about safety, consent, and caregiving?
* How do you want to talk with them now, possibly as co-parents or adults caring for aging family, about trust and responsibility?

Chapter 10

TRAUMA-INFORMED PARENTING

Parenting has a unique way of unearthing our own past experiences, often in unexpected ways. Trauma-informed parenting helps us navigate how our histories, whether marked by significant traumas or subtler wounds, can influence the way we respond to our children. By recognizing these influences, we can approach parenting with greater self-awareness, compassion, and intention, breaking cycles of reactivity and fostering connection. This approach doesn't just benefit our children; it also supports our healing, offering opportunities to create healthier emotional patterns and a more secure foundation for the next generation.

From a psychological perspective, trauma refers to any experience that overwhelms our capacity to cope, where we didn't have much choice or control, and leaves a lasting imprint on our sense of safety, identity, or connection. Trauma can take many forms and is often divided into two categories: "Big T" and "small t" traumas.

* "Big T" trauma encompasses major, life-altering events, such as abuse, neglect, or the loss of a caregiver. For example, a parent who expe-

rienced physical abuse as a child might carry deep-seated fears of confrontation, which can influence how they approach discipline or conflict with their children.

* "Small t" trauma refers to subtler, cumulative experiences that still leave a mark on our emotional landscape, such as repeated invalidation, parental criticism, or feeling overlooked. A child who grew up with a caregiver who dismissed their emotions with phrases like "stop crying, it's not a big deal" might later struggle to validate their own feelings or their child's emotions.

Both types of trauma can shape how we view ourselves and the world. Our nervous system, which governs our fight, flight, freeze, and fawn (people-pleasing) responses, is particularly impacted by trauma. When faced with reminders of these past experiences, like a child's loud cries, a moment of perceived defiance, or even the chaos of everyday parenting, our nervous system can interpret these events as threats, triggering an automatic response. These trauma triggers can lead to intense reactions such as yelling, shutting down, or feeling disproportionately overwhelmed, often leaving us wondering why we reacted so strongly.

Trauma also deeply affects emotional regulation, which is critical in parenting. Research shows that unresolved trauma can heighten stress responses, making it more difficult to remain calm in challenging moments. For example, a parent with a history of neglect may find it especially hard to tolerate their child's neediness, feeling suffocated or resentful without understanding why. Similarly, a parent who was shamed for making mistakes as a child might struggle to offer their child grace in moments of imperfection.

However, trauma-informed parenting offers a path forward. It helps us recognize when we are operating from a place of old wounds rather than the present moment, allowing us to shift from reactive to intentional responses. By addressing and working through our unresolved pain, we can better model emotional regulation and create a secure environment where our children feel safe, valued, and understood.

Why Trauma-Informed Parenting Matters

Trauma-informed parenting matters because it enables us to stop the cycle of pain from being passed down to the next generation. When we carry unresolved trauma, we may unintentionally mirror the patterns we experienced, even when we desperately want to do things differently. For example:

- A parent who experienced frequent criticism might find themselves being overly critical of their child's academic or social achievements, even as they fear becoming the same kind of parent they had.
- A parent who grew up in a household where emotions were dismissed might struggle to hold space for their child's big feelings, resorting to dismissive or reactive responses that echo their upbringing.

Trauma-informed parenting invites us to approach both ourselves, our partners, and our children with empathy, helping to rewire these ingrained patterns. By learning to recognize our triggers and respond with intention, we teach our children that emotions can be expressed safely, that mistakes are opportunities for growth, and that connection is not contingent on perfection.

This approach fosters secure attachment, where children feel free to express their needs without fear of rejection or judgment. It also allows parents to begin reparenting themselves, offering the compassion, patience, and understanding they might not have received in childhood. This dual process of healing and parenting creates a family culture rooted in safety and connection, breaking cycles of shame and fear that often linger through generations.

In this chapter, we'll explore how trauma-informed parenting can support your relationship with your child and with yourself. We'll discuss strategies to identify and navigate emotional triggers, develop healthy coping mechanisms, and model emotional resilience for your children. Whether you're parenting an infant, a teenager, or an adult child, these tools are designed to meet you where you are and support you in building a family culture of empathy, growth, and connection. Parenting through a trauma-informed lens is not about perfection; it's about progress. Together, we'll work to stop intergenerational cycles of pain and create a space where healing thrives.

Reflecting on How Your Upbringing Affects Parenting

Becoming a parent has a way of pulling old patterns to the surface, especially ones we thought we had left behind. For me, the role I slipped into most easily was the "good girl," the one who anticipates, has no needs that require attention, smooths things over, and keeps the peace. Growing up, I learned early that safety often came from tending to others' moods. If I could keep everyone calm, then I was okay too. That drive to anticipate needs and take responsibility for other people's emotions followed me into adulthood and, eventually, into motherhood.

Before kids, this dynamic didn't show up as clearly. Once I became a parent, though, it was everywhere. I became the overfunctioner. I'd tell myself I could soothe the baby faster, bathe the kids better, or manage bedtime more efficiently, so I did it all. Underneath, I was scared of what might happen if I didn't, scared my husband at the time would get overwhelmed, and scared I wouldn't know how to handle that in a man. The more I stepped in, the more he stepped back. I'd start to feel like his mom instead of his partner, and he'd start to resent me for not giving him the chance to try.

What made it more complicated was how quickly I took accountability for his reactions. If he lost patience or shut down, I'd explain it away, or validate him and abandon my needs, telling myself it was because he hadn't been taught good regulation skills or because of neurodivergency. My role became managing not only our kids' distress, but also his. And yet, beneath all the "good girl" tending, there was resentment building in me too. I wanted him to step up, but I was the one constantly stepping in.

Through therapy, both on my own and with him, I've had to face how much control I was holding on to, and how much of that came from my childhood masks. The "good girl" who thought keeping the peace was the same thing as love. The "miss independent" who convinced herself she didn't need help. The "rescuer" who felt safest when others needed saving. Each of those roles made me feel secure in the moment, but they also kept me from being equal with my partner. They left me exhausted and him diminished.

Parenting has become the mirror that shows me when those masks are running the show. I am slowly realizing (with intentional effort and conscious choice) that my kids don't need me to orchestrate a perfect environment where no one ever feels distress. Instead, what they need are parents who can share the load, even if it gets messy.

Letting my ex-husband find his own rhythm with the kids has become its own practice in trust. Releasing control still doesn't come naturally to me, but I'm learning. I'm learning that my job isn't to manage both homes or make sure everything runs perfectly. My job is to show up fully where I am, to model steadiness, to create safety, and to trust that my children have what they need in both spaces. Part of that learning has been recognizing that I'm not the whole problem here. For a long time, I carried the story that if I just worked harder, communicated better, or softened more, everything would fall into place. But the truth is, my ex was avoidant in his own ways, hesitant to bring things up or face conflict, and that dynamic shaped how we lost and now redefine our relationship. He's doing his own work to grow into a different version of himself, just as I am. I'm realizing that I can't control his process, only how I show up in mine. Co-parenting has taught me to release the idea that being "good" means being everywhere or fixing everything. Sometimes it means stepping back, allowing both of us to parent differently, and trusting that growth can happen on parallel paths.

It hasn't been easy, but little by little, I'm letting go of the idea that being "good" means doing it all. My partner and I are working on meeting each other as equals, not in a dynamic of mother and child, overfunctioner and underfunctioner, but as two people who can share the weight of raising a family. And in doing that, I'm starting to rewrite what "good" really means for me: not being endlessly selfless, but being present, authentic, and willing to trust others to carry their part too.

Resource: *In What Happened to You?* by Oprah Winfrey and Dr. Bruce Perry, readers are invited to examine how early experiences shape current reactions, especially in parenting. It offers a trauma-informed lens on why our nervous systems react the way they do, and how revisiting the past can shift the way we show up with our children.

Alongside that, *Liberated Love* by Mark Groves and Kylie McBeath explores how childhood patterns of overfunctioning, caretaking, or shutting down can play out in adult relationships, especially when stress runs high in parenting. Both resources remind us that unlearning these dynamics helps create space for more equal, connected relationships at home.

PRE-CHILD PLANNING: **Exploring the Emotional Blueprint You Bring to Parenting**

- What aspects of your childhood felt emotionally safe, and what didn't?
- How did your parents or caregivers handle stress, conflict, or big emotions?
- Are there patterns you want to carry forward, and ones do you hope to break?
- How do you imagine responding when your future child pushes boundaries or has a meltdown?
- In what ways do your upbringing and your partner's differ? How might that show up when you parent together?
- How can you support each other in pausing and reflecting, especially in moments that feel triggering?

DURING PREGNANCY: **Preparing for Emotional Triggers and Partner Dynamics**

- What kinds of emotional responses have already started to show up during pregnancy, toward your partner, your own body, or the future?
- What does "staying regulated" mean to you? How have you learned (or not learned) to do that?

* Are there specific phrases or behaviors you remember from childhood that you don't want to repeat?
* What support do you need from your partner when you feel overwhelmed or anxious?
* How does your communication change when you're both tired, stressed, or uncertain?
* Are there any unresolved emotions you want to work through before becoming a parent?

POSTPARTUM: **Rewriting Old Patterns with Self-Compassion and Awareness**

* When you feel overwhelmed, what automatic reactions or old coping patterns show up, and where might they come from?
* Are you trying to "keep the peace" or hold everything together in ways that silence your own needs or emotions?
* What does it stir in you when your baby cries, struggles to settle, or needs you constantly? Do you feel pressure to "get it right"?
* How do you speak to yourself when you make parenting mistakes, and are you offering yourself the same kindness you'd give a friend?
* What helps you repair emotionally after a moment you're not proud of, whether with your baby, your partner, or yourself?
* How does your partner respond to stress differently from you, and how can you support each other without escalating tension?

TODDLER YEARS: **Balancing Boundaries and Self-Regulation**

* When your toddler melts down, do you feel more shame, anger, or helplessness?

* Do you ever find yourself parenting in a way that feels automatic or familiar from childhood?
* What are you afraid might happen if you let go of control in difficult moments?
* How do you and your partner handle parenting disagreements in front of your child?
* What makes it hard for you to tolerate public tantrums or defiance?
* How do you want to respond differently when you feel yourself getting reactive?

4–8 YEARS: **Supporting Growth Without Repeating Harm**

* How do you handle it when your child's behavior embarrasses you in front of others?
* Do you notice yourself expecting your child to be "better behaved" than is realistic for their age?
* What do you believe about discipline, and where did those beliefs come from?
* When your child makes a mistake, do you move toward teaching or shaming, intentionally or unintentionally?
* How do you want to handle apologies and repair in your home?
* What tools help you recognize when you're reacting from old wounds rather than present needs?

9–12 YEARS: **Staying Present While Past Patterns Reemerge**

* When your preteen expresses a strong opinion or pushes back, how does that affect you?
* What old family patterns show up when there's conflict or defiance in your home?

* Do you struggle to give your child more independence? Why or why not?
* Are there fears you carry about your child's future that come from your past experiences?
* What conversations do you find yourself avoiding, and what do you worry might happen if you have them?
* How can you model emotional regulation when you're frustrated or feeling powerless?

TEENAGERS: **Trusting, Guiding, and Letting Go**

* What do you find hardest about letting your teen make their own choices?
* Do you recognize when you're parenting from fear rather than trust?
* How did your parents respond to your independence or mistakes, and how is that shaping your reactions now?
* What does respectful guidance look like to you, and are you practicing it?
* How do you show up for hard conversations with your teen instead of shutting them down?
* Are you able to apologize and repair with your teen when you miss the mark?

ADULT CHILDREN: **Reflecting on Growth, Regret, and Ongoing Connection**

* What do you hope your children remember about the way you showed up for them?
* Are there things you wish you'd done differently, and have you shared those reflections with them?
* How do you stay connected to your adult child while respecting their autonomy?

* What parts of your parenting are you most proud of? What parts still need healing?

Understanding How Past Trauma Influences Emotional Regulation

Many of us enter parenthood with every intention of staying calm, patient, and grounded. But in the heat of the moment, like when a child is yelling, clinging, hitting, or simply refusing to listen, those intentions can feel like they vanish. What shows up instead might be a raised voice, a shut-down silence, or a sense of panic that feels out of proportion to what's happening. This is often a sign that our nervous system has shifted into survival mode, not because we're broken or bad at parenting, but because we were wired this way a long time ago.

Our nervous system is designed to detect safety or threat. If, in childhood, big emotions were met with anger, punishment, emotional withdrawal, or chaos, our bodies learned to treat those emotions, ours or others', as dangerous. So, when our child melts down or our partner raises their voice, we might react as if we're under attack, even if we *know* we're not. The body doesn't always differentiate between past and present. It just tries to protect us.

I remember one morning when our preschooler was having a full-body tantrum because I gave him the blue cup instead of the red one. I was already stretched thin after a late night and an early wake-up, and I had an anxious pit in my stomach I couldn't quite place. As he screamed and flung his body onto the floor, I could feel my chest tightening and my jaw clenching. Part of me wanted to scoop him up and hold him close, but another part of me wanted to flee the room or yell, "Enough!" I stood frozen for a moment, flooded, and I ended up doing the latter. What I realized later was that my nervous system wasn't just responding to *him*; it was responding to a lifetime of learning that loud emotions lead to conflict, shame, or rejection. This is where emotional regulation meets trauma and attachment. If you grew up in a home where emotional expression was shut down, shamed, or felt unsafe, your system might be wired for hypervigilance or avoidance. For some, this shows up as an anxious-attachment response: moving in quickly to fix, smooth over, or keep everyone happy, often at the expense of your own needs. For others, it might look more avoidant: pulling away, detaching, or going quiet when things escalate.

In parenting, these patterns can get activated daily. A child crying might register as an emergency, triggering panic or resentment. A partner setting a boundary might feel like rejection or abandonment. And in moments of stress, like being "touched out" (the feeling of being overwhelmed or drained from constant physical contact after long days of holding, breastfeeding, co-sleeping, or simply having little ones climbing onto us), sleep-deprived, or emotionally depleted, our nervous system's capacity shrinks even more. In that moment with my son, I took a breath and sat down beside him. I reminded myself quietly: *This is not an emergency. I am not in danger. He is not my past.* I didn't do it perfectly, my voice was sharper than I would've liked, and I felt tension buzzing through my body. Later, once we were both calmer, we talked about it. "You were so frustrated because I gave you the wrong cup color, and I felt overwhelmed. I'm sorry I yelled. We both had a hard moment." These moments won't always look clean or gentle, but they matter. Not because we avoid rupture, but because we repair. When we can name what's happening in us and show our children that even big emotions can be held with safety and honesty, we're doing something powerful: We're helping them build a different nervous system map than the one we inherited. And when we bring our partners into these conversations, it helps too. "I noticed I shut down when we were arguing yesterday. That's something I learned to do growing up." Or "When you raised your voice, I got triggered, and I think it's because it reminded me of past moments that felt scary." These are the kinds of honest reflections that build trust, deepen connection, and slowly help rewrite old wiring.

Resource: *Good Inside* by Dr. Becky Kennedy brings a compassionate approach, encouraging parents to see themselves and their children as inherently "good" while managing emotional responses with empathy.

PRE-CHILD PLANNING: **Nervous System Check-Ins and Old Triggers**

- What situations tend to make you feel out of control or flooded, especially around noise, mess, or conflict?
- When you imagine a future child having a tantrum, what physical reactions do you notice in your body?
- What did safety feel like in your childhood? What did it sound like, look like, or smell like?
- How do you currently move through stress? Do you shut down, snap, overexplain, distract yourself?
- When your partner or close friend expresses distress, do you feel responsible, disconnected, or frozen?
- What helps your body feel grounded after intense emotion or overstimulation?

DURING PREGNANCY: **Regulation, Body Memory, and Anticipatory Stress**

* What memories or body sensations have resurfaced during pregnancy that caught you off guard?
* How do you know you're starting to dysregulate? What early signs show up in your breathing, posture, or tone?
* How do you feel when you witness someone else cry, yell, or collapse emotionally? What does that bring up?
* Are there caregiving scenarios you already anticipate feeling "too much" for you? Why those ones?
* How do you feel when people offer help or emotional support: relieved, wary, suspicious, overwhelmed?
* What's one self-soothing practice you want to try when you feel overstimulated or emotionally reactive?

POSTPARTUM: **Navigating Overwhelm, Sensory Triggers, and the Need for Space**

* What physical cues show up when you feel overstimulated or touched out or have tight shoulders, irritability, or a need to escape?
* What's your immediate reaction when the baby cries and you're already emotionally or physically drained?
* How do you experience your baby's emotional expressions? Do they feel neutral, triggering, or overwhelming, and what might influence that?
* Is it hard to ask for space without guilt, and what beliefs or conditioning might be feeding that discomfort?

- ✱ How does your partner or support system respond when you're overwhelmed? Do you feel seen, dismissed, or misunderstood?
- ✱ What helps you come back into regulation (movement, stillness, sound, silence), and how can you reach for that in the moment?

TODDLER YEARS: **Recognizing Triggers and Shifting the Energy**

- ✱ When your toddler yells, hits, or resists, what story do you start to tell yourself about your parenting?
- ✱ What kinds of toddler behavior feel disproportionately activating or personal to you?
- ✱ How does your body tell you you're entering a stress response: hot face, clenched fists, or tunnel vision?
- ✱ When you reflect later, what part of you was most activated: your fear, shame, or need for control?
- ✱ What is your first instinct when chaos erupts: fix it, flee, freeze, or confront?
- ✱ What helps you interrupt a reactive moment before it escalates?

4–8 YEARS: **Relating to Big Feelings Without Getting Pulled Under**

- ✱ When your child's emotions explode, do you feel more annoyed, threatened, helpless, or something else?
- ✱ What was your role in childhood when things got loud or messy: peacemaker, rebel, or ghost?
- ✱ How does it feel when your child disregards your instruction or emotionally withdraws from you?

* When your child recovers from a meltdown faster than you do, what does that bring up in you?
* Are you able to return to connection after conflict, or do you tend to stay distant?
* How do you use rhythm, play, or movement to regulate together after a tough moment?

9–12 YEARS: **Emotional Distance, Power Shifts, and Attachment Activation**

* When your preteen rolls their eyes or says, "You don't get it," how do you feel: hurt, defensive, or numb?
* Do you experience their emotional independence as healthy or as a threat to connection?
* Are you aware of moments when your child's emotions remind you of someone from your past (e.g., a sibling, parent, or even yourself)?
* When you feel triggered by disrespect or defiance, what's the old story you're reacting to?
* Do you go into fix-it mode, silent treatment, sarcasm, or overexplaining when you feel emotionally rejected?
* How do you want to respond differently when you feel dismissed or disrespected?

TEENAGERS: **Letting Go Without Losing Regulation**

* When your teen is withdrawn or explosive, what attachment fears show up in you?
* Do you read their distancing as personal rejection or as normal boundary-building?
* What kind of emotional control do you try to assert, and how does it usually land?

- Are you able to regulate during hard conversations, or only afterward in reflection?
- What narratives do you still carry about authority, obedience, or emotional maturity from your upbringing?
- What helps you stay in a state of connection, even when you disagree or disconnect?

ADULT CHILDREN: **Repair, Reflection, and Relearning Regulation Together**

- Are there moments from their childhood you still carry guilt or confusion about? Have you talked about them?
- Do you notice any nervous system responses (e.g., tension, bracing, shutdown) when difficult topics come up with your adult child?
- What emotional habits from early parenting still show up in your dynamic today?
- How do you respond when they express hurt, boundaries, or criticism? Are you able to stay open?
- What kind of relationship do you want now, and how can you regulate yourself to support that vision?
- What does co-regulation look like between adults? How do you repair, soften, and reconnect?

Raising Children Without Parentification

Many adults come into therapy with a quiet but persistent sense of fatigue, an exhaustion that seems like it's coming from overwork or burnout in the present but has its roots deeper in childhood, in roles that were hard to hold. This is often the result of parentification, a dynamic where a child becomes responsible for meeting a parent's emotional or practical needs. Sometimes this shows up as a child being the emotional anchor in the home: soothing an overwhelmed parent, mediating adult conflict, or offering comfort during financial or relational instability. Other times, it's more concrete: making meals, cleaning, raising siblings, or contributing financially to help the family survive.

It's important to note that these roles aren't always born out of emotional neglect. In many homes, especially single-parent households, families with mental or physical health challenges, or underprivileged families, the survival of the entire unit depends on shared responsibility. A child stepping up might not be explicitly asked to; they just see the gaps and fill them. And in some cultures, these expectations are normalized or even idealized. It might be expected that older children care for siblings, or that grown children later care for aging parents who move into the family home. These intergenerational values can hold deep meaning and purpose. But when not balanced with emotional boundaries and a child's developmental needs, they can also blur the lines of where care becomes obligation, and where love gets tangled with resentment.

Parentification becomes harmful when a child's worth starts to hinge on how useful or emotionally available they are to others. When "being good" means not causing trouble, staying quiet, anticipating everyone's needs, or keeping the peace. Over time, these coping strategies can harden into identity. What begins as *parent-pleasing* often matures into *people-pleasing*, and in trauma therapy, we often refer to this as *fawning*: the compulsion to stay safe by over-accommodating others, fearing conflict, and pushing your needs down, even when it costs you your well-being. Fawning is an adaptive survival response. It can show up in adult relationships as chronic over-giving, struggling to express needs, or resentment that simmers under a polite exterior. It can lead someone to tolerate mistreatment, avoid conflict at all costs, or feel crushed by guilt when they finally say no. It can even show up in parenting, where someone might over-function, over-apologize, or tiptoe around their child's feelings because any sign of disapproval or chaos feels unbearable.

As parents, especially those who were once the "responsible child," it can be hard to unlearn the belief that being needed equals being loved. However, raising emotionally healthy children means learning to tolerate our discomfort without passing it down. It means not leaning on our kids to fill our emotional voids, not using them as confidants or sounding boards for personal or non-age appropriate matters, and not rewarding them for growing up too fast just because it makes things easier for us. This doesn't mean abandoning cultural values around family care or closeness, but it does mean being thoughtful about how we preserve those values *without* expecting children to carry adult-sized burdens. It means recognizing that love, care, and responsibility can all exist within boundaries that protect a child's right to stay a child. To do this, we need to ask: Are we venting to our child when we really need to talk to a partner, friend, or therapist? Are we asking them to hold emotions they don't have the tools to process? Are we over-relying on them to manage the mood of the household? These questions are designed to foster awareness. When we stay curious and take ownership of our healing, we permit our children to have choice—choice and freedom to grow into empathetic, caring adults who help others not because they were expected to, but because they had space to develop a true, healthy sense of self.

Resource: In *Boundaries: When to Say Yes, How to Say No to Take Control of Your Life*, Dr. Henry Cloud and Dr. John Townsend discuss the essential role of boundaries in all relationships. For parents, the book offers strategies to create healthy emotional boundaries that support children's development, allowing them to grow up feeling secure, empathic, and free to explore their own emotions without the weight of adult concerns.

PRE-CHILD PLANNING: **Unpacking Responsibility, Cultural Norms, and Emotional Labor**

* Was it expected in your family or culture that children contribute emotionally or practically to household survival?
* Did you feel like you had to earn love by being helpful, responsible, or emotionally attuned?
* How do you define being a "good child," and how might that shape your parenting ideals?
* Are there unspoken expectations that you might pass down (e.g., "good kids don't complain," "family comes first no matter what")?
* How can your partner and you support each other in setting boundaries with extended family, especially when cultural obligations are strong?
* What emotional roles did you take on in childhood, and which ones do you want to release before parenting?

DURING PREGNANCY: **Recognizing Old Patterns and Building Support Networks**

* When you feel vulnerable or stressed, who do you instinctively turn to. Do you expect to turn to your child in the future?
* Are there beliefs you hold around sacrifice or suffering in parenthood that may be rooted in how you were raised?

* How do you feel about asking for help from peers or community members? Does it feel safe or shameful?
* What kinds of emotional care did you miss growing up that you hope to give your child, and are you also giving it to yourself?
* How does your culture or upbringing influence who's "supposed" to support the parent emotionally?
* Who can you build into your adult emotional care team now, so you're not unconsciously leaning on your child later?

POSTPARTUM: **Staying Grounded in Early Emotional Needs**

* When you feel alone or depleted, do you feel guilty for needing support, or do you reach for it freely?
* Do you talk to your baby in ways that soothe you more than them? What need might that be filling?
* How can you tell the difference between connection and emotional dependency with your infant?
* Are there signs you're seeking validation or comfort from your child's behavior or responses?
* How can you create rituals of support (a text check-in, a postpartum circle, a quiet moment alone) that don't involve your child?
* If you grew up needing to care for adults, how can you allow yourself to be cared for now?

TODDLER YEARS: **Modeling Boundaries and Emotional Ownership**

* When your toddler cries or resists, do you feel rejected or like you've failed in some way?

* Do you narrate your emotions in a way that helps them understand, or in a way that seeks their comfort?
* How do you respond when your toddler shows concern for you? Do you reassure them or let them carry it?
* Are there moments when you praise them more for "helping" you than just being themselves?
* Are you more comfortable with them being quiet and compliant than expressing their needs? Why?
* How can you show your toddler that you can hold both their big feelings and your own without needing them to fix anything?

4–8 YEARS: **Teaching Emotional Responsibility Without Overloading**

* When your child shows emotional sensitivity, do you nurture that gently or start to rely on it?
* Do you catch yourself saying things like, "That really helped Mommy feel better" too often?
* Are there ways you encourage emotional caretaking in your child because it feels nice, even if it's too much?
* How did your family treat "good kids," and is that story influencing how you praise or correct your child now?
* How do you respond when your child worries about you? Do you allow them to return to play, or keep them emotionally involved?
* Are there community or cultural narratives (e.g., "eldest daughters raise the family") that you need to actively challenge?

9–12 YEARS: **Balancing Maturity with Protection from Adult Stress**

* Do you ever find yourself venting about adult issues (money, relationships, family conflict) to your preteen?
* When they ask questions about family stress, do you answer with context or emotional detail they're not ready for?
* How do you feel when your child takes on responsibilities beyond their age?
* What messages do they hear about self-sacrifice or putting others first in their home or culture?
* How do you model rest, play, or boundary-setting? Are you showing them it's okay not to be productive or helpful all the time?
* Do you see their empathy as a strength and protect them from feeling responsible for everyone?

TEENAGERS: **Creating Space for Identity and Letting Go of Overfunctioning**

* Do you go to your teen for emotional validation or processing that would be better suited for an adult?
* Do you expect them to understand or manage your mood, even subtly?
* Have you said things to them like, "You're the only one who gets me," or "I couldn't do this without you"? What might that put on their shoulders?
* Are there cultural or generational beliefs you carry that equate being a "good child" with self-sacrifice or silence?
* When they struggle to set boundaries with others, do you wonder if they learned that from you?

* How can you encourage them to prioritize their needs without guilt or fear of letting you down?

ADULT CHILDREN: **Repairing Old Patterns and Respecting Boundaries**

* Have you ever apologized for emotional roles you placed on them that weren't theirs to carry?
* Are you still turning to them as an emotional sounding board instead of your peers or other supports?
* How do you react when they set boundaries with you? Do you feel hurt, abandoned, or proud?
* What cultural or family beliefs make it hard for you to let go of emotional dependence on them?
* Have you given them explicit permission to prioritize their well-being, even if it means stepping back from caretaking roles in the family?
* What does it look like to show love and closeness now that you are both adults, and how do you model that without pressure or guilt?

Chapter 11

CELEBRATIONS AND HOLIDAYS: FROM CONFLICT TO CONNECTION

As parents, we often feel the pressure to create meaningful, magical moments for our families. Holidays, birthdays, anniversaries, and cultural celebrations can carry so much weight, emotionally, historically, and relationally. These events are often tied to how we were raised, what we longed for, or how we hoped things would feel. For some, holidays bring up nostalgia and warmth. For others, they stir grief, resentment, or complicated family dynamics. Many of us enter parenthood hoping to create something better, more intentional, or more grounded for our children, but we don't always know how to get there.

The Psychology Behind Celebration and Conflict

Celebrations are rituals, and rituals carry deep psychological meaning. They provide a sense of identity, predictability, and belonging. But they can also bring up unresolved dynamics, highlight emotional labor imbalances, or resurface past disappointments. When people come together to raise children, they're bringing not just their memories and rituals, but also their unspoken expectations, cultural scripts, and emotional wounds.

The tension that arises around holidays can get heavy when we focus on whose needs are prioritized, whose vision is followed, and whether unspoken feelings are acknowledged or dismissed. Understanding the emotional layers behind celebration can help parents and caregivers have more honest conversations, reduce resentment, and foster a sense of shared intention.

Why Talking About Holidays and Celebrations Matters

When we avoid talking about how holidays feel to us, or when we power through them on autopilot, we miss an opportunity to build intimacy, collaboration, and joy. Conversations about celebration are actually conversations about:

* emotional labor
* cultural identity, religion, community, and values
* grief and unmet needs
* privilege and accessibility
* parenting philosophy
* boundaries and inclusion

This chapter invites you to explore how holidays and celebrations affect your family emotionally, logistically, and relationally. It's a chance to name what feels good, what feels hard, and what might need to shift. Whether you grew up with elaborate traditions or none at all, these conversations can help you redefine connection on your own terms. Whether it's Christmas or Eid, Mother's Day or a birthday, or a nontraditional holiday your family holds dear, you deserve a celebration that feels mutual and meaningful.

The Pressure to Perform During Holidays

Holidays often come with this invisible pressure, the pressure to make everything feel magical, meaningful, and memorable. Whether it's the perfectly set table, the coordinated outfits, or the expectation that everyone will somehow just get along for one day, so many of us carry around a mental picture of how holidays are *supposed* to look. For me, that picture was shaped by years of Slovak Christmas Eve dinners: the same familiar dishes every year, the quiet of the house after cooking all day, and the moment we lit the first candle on the table. We'd start with *oblátky* (wafers) drizzled with honey and garlic, then *kapustnica* (sauerkraut soup), fried carp or fish fillets, and a big bowl of homemade potato salad. It was ritualistic in the best way, predictable, warm, grounding. I loved that meal so much it felt almost sacred.

So, naturally, when I became a parent, I wanted to re-create that same sense of occasion for my own family. I pictured my kids sitting still at the table, sampling each dish, asking questions about where the recipes came from. I imagined a soft kind of holiday magic, one that would link them back to their roots and also bring us closer together. When we got to my parents' place for dinner that one Christmas evening, the table was set just as I remembered, and I sat us all down around the table ready for our tradition to continue as usual, but the evening didn't go as I had pictured. My son wanted nothing to do with the food. He was overstimulated, overtired, and uninterested. He kept climbing out of his chair, wandering around, asking for snacks that weren't on the menu, and fixating on a toy he'd opened earlier that day. I spent most of the meal trying to coax him back to the table and keep the plates from ending up on the floor. I was flustered, frustrated, and trying to keep it together, mostly because

I'd put so much pressure on myself for this moment to feel special, and when it didn't, I felt like I had failed at something I couldn't quite name. My daughter sat in her chair and played with her food joyfully, so the attention was more focused on my son at the time.

At some point during cleanup, my mom gently said, "It's going to look different for him right now, and that's okay. He has so much he can play with and it's okay that he didn't dive into the food like you and your sister would." She wasn't judging me, just reminding me that tradition isn't a performance. It's a connection point, not a script. When I really thought about it, I realized that what made those dinners feel special growing up wasn't how well-behaved we were or whether every course was served perfectly. It was the feeling of togetherness, even if we were tired or cranky or not eating everything on our plates.

There's still a part of me that wants to "get it right." I don't think that feeling ever fully disappears. But now, I try to notice when that performance energy is creeping in, and then ask myself whether it's really about the people at the table or the version of myself I think I should be. Holidays are already emotionally loaded, and adding the pressure to make them perfect only makes them harder. What I want now is for my kids to look back and remember that holidays felt safe, flexible, and full of warmth, even if they ate cereal for dinner or skipped the soup.

Resource: *Simplicity Parenting* by Kim John Payne explores how too much stuff, too many choices, and too much pressure can overwhelm children and families. He encourages parents to slow down, create simple rhythms, and focus on connection over perfection. It's a helpful reminder that holiday magic doesn't come from doing more; it comes from feeling safe, grounded, and present.

PRE-CHILD PLANNING: **Exploring Your Personal Holiday Histories**

* What holidays or traditions did your family celebrate growing up? How did your cultural background or religion shape those?
* Were there expectations around gender roles, gifts, or emotional performance (e.g., pretending to be happy)?
* What holiday rituals gave you a sense of belonging, and which ones felt like pressure?
* If you imagine parenting through the holidays, what are you excited about? Nervous about?
* What would it mean to create traditions that reflect your shared values instead of defaulting to what was modeled for you?

DURING PREGNANCY: **Setting Foundations for Your Family Culture**

* What traditions or events are coming up that you may want to rethink or approach differently this year?
* How do you want to include or limit extended family during the holidays?
* Are there specific cultural or spiritual practices you want to bring into your child's life?
* What pressures do you feel to make things look or feel a certain way, and where are those coming from?
* What is one gentle, meaningful ritual you can begin now that aligns with who you are becoming as parents?

POSTPARTUM: **Reimagining the Holidays with Realistic Expectations**

* What's actually doable this year, given your sleep, capacity, and emotional bandwidth?
* How do you grieve the gap between what you hoped for and what's possible right now?
* How do you protect this early chapter with quiet, intentional time?
* What are you doing because you feel obligated, and what might you do differently if you gave yourself permission to?
* How do you share the load of planning, hosting, or even declining invitations?

TODDLER YEARS: **Navigating Excitement and Overload**

* How do you set up holiday routines that help your toddler feel secure and grounded?
* What kinds of traditions make sense for their age, attention span, and sensory needs?
* Are there moments when you're doing something for appearances rather than connection?
* What's a holiday moment that brought joy to your child, and to you?
* How do you teach about gratitude, giving, or family without pressure?

4–8 YEARS: **Building Meaning Through Ritual**

* What are your kids learning about culture, family, and giving through your holiday choices?
* Are there school or community traditions that you want to participate in—or opt out of?
* How do you handle questions about why you do (or don't do) certain things?

* What feels performative versus connected?
* How do you ensure the mental and emotional labor isn't falling on just one partner?

9–12 YEARS: **Identity, Inclusion, and Belonging**

* What are they starting to notice about how you celebrate compared to others (friends, media, community)?
* How can you include them in the planning or decision-making in small, age-appropriate ways?
* Are there family dynamics (e.g., favoritism, gender roles, religious expectations) they're picking up on and trying to make sense of?
* What kinds of traditions help them feel connected to culture or heritage, and which ones feel confusing or burdensome?
* How do you talk to them about being part of a mixed-faith, mixed-culture, or blended family when it comes to rituals and expectations?
* Are you modeling the kind of emotional honesty you hope they'll carry into their future holidays?

TEENAGERS: **Flexing with Change**

* What traditions do they still want to be a part of, and what are they outgrowing?
* How do you balance nostalgia with letting them have more agency?
* Are you making assumptions about what matters to them based on what mattered to you?
* How do you talk openly about your hopes for holidays while leaving room for new rhythms?
* What can you let go of to make space for shared connection?

ADULT CHILDREN: **Letting Go, Reconnecting Differently**

* Are you clinging to traditions or timelines that no longer serve your relationships?
* How do you offer invitations instead of obligations?
* How do you welcome their partners, chosen families, or different spiritual practices?
* What are your hopes for feeling connected during holidays without forcing a particular structure?

Celebrations When You Feel Left Out or Let Down

There's something incredibly tender about special days, birthdays, anniversaries, cultural celebrations, and even holidays like Valentine's Day. These days can hold so much hope, pressure, and emotion, especially for the parent who's carrying most of the invisible labor in the family. Whether it's doing the behind-the-scenes planning, thinking of everyone's needs, coordinating schedules, or simply holding the emotional tone of the day, the weight of making things "feel special" often falls on one person, and more often than not, that person is the mom.

We don't always talk about how complicated it can feel to be the one holding everything, and then not feeling held in return. What I've noticed in my own life, and in conversations with other parents, is that a lot of disappointment around holidays doesn't come from unreasonable expectations. It comes from the quiet hope that someone will *see* how much we do without being asked. That someone will say, "You've done enough, let me take this one," or "Here, I have planned it out so the kids are taken care of, and you don't have to worry about them, so you can do xyz." In the absence of clear conversations, these hopes can go unnoticed. Resentments build. And the day that was supposed to be fun or celebratory ends up feeling heavy.

In our home, one tradition that's stuck, and that I really love, is what we do for birthdays. We surprise the birthday person first thing in the morning by barging into their room with breakfast, singing loudly, and handing them presents right in bed. It's chaotic and joyful and very much our own. The kids have started taking the lead now, helping bring breakfast, making cards, and getting way too excited about waking each other up early. At the same time, I'm deeply aware that not all holidays feel joyful or easy for everyone. Some people feel left out because the holiday they celebrate isn't acknowledged in their community or school. Others are carrying grief about who's not there, about what's changed, or about what they never got to have. And in multicultural, interfaith, or blended families, these days can bring up questions about which traditions get prioritized and why. What's helped in our family is naming it all: the expectations, the hopes, the fears, the longing. We've learned to check in ahead of time about what each person might need or want in hopes of reducing the guesswork.

Resource: If you've ever found yourself feeling resentful or quietly disappointed on a day you hoped would feel special, *Drop the Ball* by Tiffany Dufu is a thoughtful and empowering read. It explores how so many of us carry the emotional weight of holidays and milestones without naming what we need and how learning to ask for help (and actually let it happen) can be an act of self-respect and deeper connection.

PRE-CHILD PLANNING: **Reflecting on What We Learned Growing Up**

* What messages did you grow up with about what gets celebrated and how? Were there certain

holidays or milestones that mattered more than others in your family or culture?

* As a child or teen, did you see one parent (often the mom) doing most of the planning and not getting much in return? How did that shape your understanding of roles in celebration?
* Were there unspoken rules around "not asking for too much" or needing to act happy even if you felt disappointed or unseen?
* When you think of Valentine's Day, Mother's/Father's Day, or birthdays, what emotional memories come up? Were you taught to expect grand gestures, or was love shown quietly, or maybe not at all?
* In your friendships or community now, do you see certain people (especially women or caregivers) being overlooked or expected to "just know" what to do? How do you want to shift that narrative in your own life?
* How do we want to approach celebrations in a way that acknowledges effort, spreads responsibility, and values each person, not just on their "special" day, but regularly?

DURING PREGNANCY: **Acknowledging Tenderness and Identity Shifts**

* Are there any holidays this year that feel more emotionally charged now that you're preparing for parenthood?
* Do you want to be acknowledged as a parent already, even before the baby is here? If so, what would feel meaningful to you?
* How are your changing roles, as partner, expectant parent, or family member shaping what you need from others during holidays?

- Are there subtle ways you could include others (like grandparents, chosen family, or friends) in supporting you during this transition?
- What do you wish people understood about the emotional work of becoming a parent, even before the baby arrives?

POSTPARTUM: **Emotional Labor and Invisible Work**

- Who is quietly carrying the emotional load of planning, organizing, or making holidays happen, and is that work being noticed?
- Are there unspoken resentments building because one of you feels forgotten, underappreciated, or emotionally depleted?
- Have you communicated clearly about what kind of support or acknowledgment you need, or are you hoping the other will just "get it"?
- What would it look like to create a gentler, more reciprocal approach to celebrating milestones right now?
- If a recent celebration left one of you feeling hurt or unseen, how can you revisit it with compassion and curiosity?

TODDLER YEARS: **Shared Effort, Shared Appreciation**

- As your days get fuller and more chaotic, are you making time to check in with each other about how you're doing emotionally, especially around holidays?
- Are your own needs getting brushed aside in the rush to make holidays feel "magical" for your toddler?

* What could you do (big or small) to show appreciation to one another during birthday weeks, cultural holidays, or even just everyday routines?
* Is one of you always behind the camera, cleaning up, or planning, but rarely in the spotlight?
* How can you start modeling celebration and gratitude as a family value, not just a seasonal thing?

4–8 YEARS: **Teaching and Practicing Mutual Respect**

* What are your kids starting to learn by watching how adults in their lives are appreciated (or not) on holidays and special days?
* Are there assumptions forming about who plans, who gives, and who gets? How can you challenge those?
* Are there ways to involve them in simple but meaningful acts of kindness, like writing a thank-you card, planning a surprise, or talking about emotional labor?
* How do you talk to your kids about inclusivity and fairness when someone feels left out (whether it's a parent, a sibling, or someone in their class)?
* What language can you use to help them understand that effort deserves acknowledgment, and that love can be shown in many forms?

9–12 YEARS: **Visibility, Fairness, and Emotional Learning**

* Are your kids starting to notice and ask questions about who does what around holidays? Are you open to those conversations?

* Have you invited them to think about what makes someone feel seen or appreciated, not just on birthdays or Valentine's Day, but in daily life?
* Are you talking openly about how not everyone celebrates the same holidays, and how being thoughtful and inclusive can make a big difference?
* Have you shared your feelings, past or present, about times you felt left out, and how you've learned to speak up or make changes?
* Can you cocreate a tradition where everyone in the family gets a chance to feel valued, including the adults?

TEENAGERS: **Navigating Distance and Emotional Complexity**

* Are you placing pressure on your teens to celebrate in ways that feel performative, or are you giving them agency and trust?
* How do you model emotional vulnerability if you're feeling unappreciated without guilt-tripping them?
* Are you making space for them to voice which holidays feel meaningful and which don't resonate for them anymore?
* How do you approach conversations about culture, community, and inclusion if they're navigating more diverse friendships or relationships?
* What values around appreciation and effort do you hope they take with them into their future relationships?

ADULT CHILDREN: **Grief, Change, and New Forms of Connection**

* Are you holding onto certain traditions out of habit, or are you adapting them in ways that work for everyone?
* Have you named the grief that can come with being less central in your children's holiday plans or milestones?
* How do you express what matters to you around being acknowledged without placing emotional weight or guilt on them?
* Are you welcoming their partners, chosen family, or different ways of celebrating with openness and curiosity?

Making Room for Grief, Loss, or Estrangement

There are some years when the holidays feel heavier than joyful, carrying that quiet, creeping weight that builds as the world celebrates, while you're just trying to hold it together. It might be fresh grief, raw and undeniable. Or it might be the softer, slower ache of something that's been missing for a long time. A person, a relationship, a version of your family that no longer exists, or maybe never quite existed the way you thought it did.

In our family, there's been a lot of movement over the years. People have come and gone, some through breakups. Family and friends have passed away, others have gone due to deep ruptures, and some just faded out. The makeup of our holiday table looks different some years, and while I've grown used to the shifts, my children haven't. They're still little, and they remember. They remember who was here last year, who brought a certain dessert, who sat next to them and helped them open their gift. And when they're not here, they notice. "Why didn't they come?" "Where did they go?" It always catches me off guard because I know that grown-up dynamics are rarely simple and often painful, and not something I can explain to kids who just miss someone they used to see at birthdays and family dinners.

So, I say, "They're not here this time," and "It's okay to miss them. What did you enjoy most about having them here?" I try to let them feel the truth of it without layering it with all of my emotions, because the truth is, I miss some of them, too. People I still love but can't be around. People who made holidays feel whole, and whose absence makes it harder to pretend everything is fine. And when I see it through their eyes, that empty seat, that soft question, I feel the pang of it all over again. This part of the chapter is for those of us who are holding grief that doesn't always get named. Who are living through the holidays while also living through loss, of a person, a connection, a version of life that no longer fits. For people navigating the distance between what they hoped for and what's actually here. For the ones who have a calendar full of events but no desire to attend. For the ones trying to make it special for their kids while carrying sadness they don't want to pass on. For the ones still figuring out how to answer, "Where did they go?" even when they're asking themselves the same thing.

Resources: If you're holding complicated grief around family rupture, two books that can be especially grounding are *The Grief Recovery Handbook* by John W. James and Russell Friedman, and *Rules of Estrangement* by Dr. Joshua Coleman. Together, they offer both emotional validation and practical tools for processing loss that doesn't always have closure. *The Grief Recovery Handbook* gently helps you name and move through the invisible weight of unspoken goodbyes, while *Rules of Estrangement* explores why family disconnection happens and how to navigate it with compassion, boundaries, and clarity, especially during emotionally loaded seasons like the holidays.

PRE-CHILD PLANNING: **Naming What Hurts and Choosing What Heals**

* What were the holidays you dreaded growing up, and why? Was it about grief, tension, pretending, or simply feeling unseen?
* Were you taught to protect the family image, to smile through the discomfort, or to downplay your needs to keep the peace?
* Were there people you missed or wished were there but weren't talked about? How did silence shape your understanding of absence?
* How did your culture or family handle difficult emotions around holidays, grief, anger, and difference? Did you feel there was room to feel them at all?
* When you picture future holidays as a parent, what do you want to protect yourself and your child from?
* Who do you imagine at your future holiday table? Are there people or kinds of connection you hope to include that weren't present for you growing up?

DURING PREGNANCY: **Holding Grief and Hope Together**

* Are there relationships or wounds that feel more present now that you're about to become a parent, especially during holidays?
* What are your fears around navigating family events with a new role and a growing identity? Are there specific tensions you want to avoid?
* Who's missing this season, by death, distance, estrangement, or circumstance, and how do you want to honor or acknowledge that?
* How can you build a ritual, even something small, that holds space for both grief and anticipation?

* Are there ways you can quietly protect your peace without needing to justify your boundaries to anyone?
* Who can you lean on emotionally during this time?

POSTPARTUM: **Protecting Tenderness and Energy**

* Which parts of the holidays feel emotionally heavy right now, and how can you give yourselves permission to step away from them?
* Is there someone you wish were here to witness this chapter, someone you've lost, drifted from, or don't feel safe reconnecting with?
* What does "celebrating" look like when you're exhausted, vulnerable, and navigating a whole new version of yourself?
* If your family of origin isn't emotionally safe, how do you want to protect your child from absorbing that dynamic?
* Are you allowed to grieve the family you thought you'd have, or the support you imagined you'd receive, while still loving the family you're building?
* What's one tiny thing you could do, just for you, that acknowledges the season without forcing it to look or feel a certain way?

TODDLER YEARS: **Simplifying, Soothing, and Showing Up Gently**

* What do you want your child to remember about this season, not in terms of gifts or events, but the emotional tone?
* Are you trying to re-create a version of the holidays you never actually got to experience? How's that landing in your body?

* How do you explain absence or change to a toddler in a way that's honest but not heavy?
* Are there traditions you're holding onto out of guilt or fear rather than joy? What would it feel like to let them go?
* What sensory, emotional, or relational needs do you have as parents right now, and how can you center those, too?
* If you're feeling sadness or grief, how do you make space to feel it without letting it swallow the whole day?

4–8 YEARS: **Talking About Absence, Inclusion, and Change**

* How do you explain why certain people no longer come around, or why you don't go to certain places, without shaming or hiding the truth?
* Are your children starting to notice that their family looks, sounds, or gathers differently from others? How do you help them feel proud of that difference?
* Can you introduce stories, media, or traditions that reflect the reality of grief, chosen family, or interfaith/mixed-culture celebrations?
* Are you naming the people or places you miss, even in simple ways like a memory jar, a candle, or drawing a picture?
* What questions are your children asking that catch you off guard, and how can you stay open even when you don't have a perfect answer?
* Who in your extended family or circle models inclusion, softness, or unconditional care, and how can you lift those voices this year?

9–12 YEARS: **Naming Feelings, Making Space for Difference**

* Are your kids starting to piece together family dynamics that you've been trying to shield them from? What's a middle ground between secrecy and oversharing?
* Have you ever asked them how they feel about your family's way of doing holidays, or if anything feels confusing, unfair, or just . . . off?
* Are they holding space for their grief (e.g., divorce, loss, estrangement), and do they know they're allowed to feel it openly?
* Can you cocreate a tradition that centers on a value, such as remembering, welcoming difference, or pausing to check in emotionally?
* How can you talk about the tension between honoring heritage and choosing something different from what was handed down?
* Are you making room for them to witness you being honest about pain or discomfort without making it their job to fix it?

TEENAGERS: **Agency, Emotional Honesty, and Mutual Respect**

* Are you making assumptions about how your teens "should" feel about holidays based on your own hopes or wounds?
* How can you invite them into honest conversations about what feels meaningful, optional, outdated, or emotionally taxing?
* Are you willing to hear that they don't enjoy certain gatherings or rituals—and to honor that with curiosity instead of guilt?
* Are they seeing you take care of yourself emotionally? Are you modeling how to set

boundaries, skip events, or grieve out loud when needed?

* If they're struggling with absence, exclusion, or identity-related tensions around family, are you actively making space for those conversations?
* What would it look like to give them some authorship over how you do holidays, rituals, stories, playlists, and acts of care?

ADULT CHILDREN: **Navigating Estrangement, Loss, and Healing**

* Are you still pretending some family dynamics are fine when they're clearly not? What conversations are long overdue, or no longer worth having?
* What do you need from holidays now that you didn't know how to ask for before? Can you voice that to each other without obligation?
* If there's someone you've lost or become estranged from, do you want to make space for their memory, or do you need space from it?
* Are you trying to fix something through tradition that would be better healed through honesty or distance?
* How can you let your adult kids take the lead on what connection looks like, even if it's quieter, shorter, or totally different?
* How can you stay connected and on the same page about the holidays if you're co-parenting from two separate homes?

Chapter 12

CONFLICT STYLES AND REPAIR AFTER FIGHTS

Conflict is inevitable in any close relationship, and it doesn't mean it's all bad, but how we move through it makes all the difference. When handled with care, conflict can deepen understanding and connection. But when it's left unresolved, it can build walls, reinforce painful patterns, and leave us feeling isolated even in the relationships that matter most. Rethinking conflict in parenthood and partnership means noticing what gets stirred up in us during a disagreement, understanding what our bodies are trying to protect, and learning how to come back to each other with care. It's about seeing conflict not as something to avoid, but as an opportunity to build trust, intimacy, and repair.

The Psychology of Conflict and Emotional Patterns

Psychologically, our approach to conflict is shaped by the early models we grew up with. If we were raised in homes where arguments were explosive or avoided, where apologies were rare or one-sided, we likely carry nervous systems that react quickly, either by shutting down or trying to fix things fast. These patterns often play out in adulthood, especially under stress, exhaustion, or emotional strain.

Research on attachment and conflict highlights how our emotional needs and regulation skills affect how we fight and how we make up. Some people pursue connection when there's tension, needing to resolve things right away. Others withdraw to protect themselves from overwhelm. These patterns, often called the pursuer-withdrawer dynamic, aren't flaws; they're strategies for safety. But when we don't understand them, they can keep us stuck in painful cycles of miscommunication and disconnection.

Understanding the role of the nervous system, trauma history, and neurodivergence can help us respond to each other with more compassion. When we know what tends to activate us, and why, we can start to shift from reactive to reflective, making space for softer moments even in the midst of conflict.

In this chapter, we'll explore where our conflict styles come from, how trauma and stress shape our responses, and how to create a culture of repair in our relationships. Whether you're navigating recurring arguments or moments of deep rupture, my hope is that these reflections and tools will help you reconnect with the parts of yourself that long for safety, understanding, and care.

Where We Learned to Fight: Family Patterns and Conflict Styles

I grew up in a home where conflict didn't make sense to me; it either simmered in silence or exploded without warning. There wasn't much in between. Some days, we tiptoed around each other, pretending nothing was wrong while the air felt heavy with everything unspoken. Other days, something small would ignite something much bigger, and everything came out at once, loud, sharp, and overwhelming. Then came the quiet again, but not the peaceful kind. It was the kind of quiet that made you second-guess every word, every glance, wondering if something else was about to snap.

It took me years to understand how much that kind of unpredictability wired my nervous system—why I still hesitate to speak up, why I replay conversations in my head a dozen times before I say a word, why someone's change in tone or the delay in a text message can make my chest tighten. I didn't know, back then, that I was learning how to survive tension, not how to move through it. The way my family handled conflict didn't begin with them; it came from intergenerational survival, from cultural norms around obedience and respect, from unspoken trauma, undiagnosed mental health challenges, and the sheer exhaustion of parenting without support. My caregivers didn't have the resources we do now. They didn't have therapy, parenting books, podcasts, or language for regulation or rupture and repair. They had their own unresolved stories and nervous systems doing their best. That doesn't mean the impact wasn't real (it absolutely was), but it helps me hold it with more compassion now. It helps me understand that the way I learned to respond to conflict—by anticipating moods, minimizing myself, or keeping the peace at any cost—was my adaptation.

And now, as a parent, I have access to tools they didn't. I have the chance to pause, to notice the script I inherited, and choose something different. I'm not always perfect at it, but I try. I am continuing to realize that when conflict is handled with intention, it doesn't always have to be something that is inherently scary or bad.

Resource: If you grew up in a home where conflict felt unsafe, unpredictable, or suffocating, *The Dance of Anger* by Harriet Lerner is a powerful read. It explores how we inherit emotional patterns, especially around silence, people-pleasing, and suppressed anger, and how we can begin speaking up for ourselves with clarity and compassion.

PRE-CHILD PLANNING: **Unpacking Our Conflict Blueprints**

* What did conflict feel like in your childhood home: tense silence, yelling, sarcasm, withdrawal, something else?
* What was your role in those moments? Were you the fixer, the avoider, the one who kept the peace, the one who fought back?
* Who was "allowed" to express anger or frustration in your home, and who wasn't?
* How might culture, gender, or generational trauma have shaped your family's conflict dynamics?
* What beliefs about conflict did you carry into adulthood, about safety, love, or worthiness?
* What parts of that legacy do you want to interrupt as a parent? What do you want to do differently?

DURING PREGNANCY: **Navigating Change and Anticipating Tension**

* Are you noticing any early signs of old conflict patterns surfacing between you and your partner now that you're under new stress?
* What have you learned about your own nervous system's response to conflict? Do you tend to freeze, appease, escalate, or withdraw?
* How did your caregivers handle conflict, and how did it affect your view of closeness, safety, or communication in relationships?

* What kind of conflict dynamic do you want to protect your future child from, and what would you like to model instead?
* What does "healthy conflict" even mean to you? Have you ever seen it modeled?

POSTPARTUM: **Treading Carefully While Exhausted and Tender**

* When conflict shows up now, does it remind you of anything from your past: old fears, familiar dynamics, or childhood scripts?
* Are you noticing inherited habits like shutting down, minimizing needs, or overexplaining? Where might those have come from?
* What feels familiar about your current reactions to tension, and what feels new or different?
* In moments of stress or disagreement, are you harder on yourself than you would be on your partner? Where did that voice begin?
* What do you want your child to internalize about emotions, voice, and safety, even when things feel hard?

TODDLER YEARS: **Modeling Emotional Safety in Real Time**

* When your child expresses anger or frustration, what comes up for you? Do you feel triggered, frozen, unsure?
* Do you see any adults in your life currently express emotions in a safe, regulated way?
* How do you react when your child disobeys or challenges you? Do any old voices or family rules echo in those moments?

* What feels hard about staying present during your toddler's emotional storms? Does it connect to your own experiences as a child?
* What are you learning about your early emotional wounds by witnessing your child's full range of feelings?

4–8 YEARS: **Teaching Conflict Without Fear**

* Do your child's big emotions stir up any memories from your own childhood, things you were shamed or punished for feeling?
* How did adults in your life respond when you were upset, overwhelmed, or scared? How does that influence your responses now?
* Are there family patterns (e.g., yelling, stonewalling, sarcasm) that you've caught yourself repeating unintentionally?
* What messages do you hope to replace, like "don't talk back" or "calm down," with something more emotionally honest?
* How are you helping your child feel what you might not have been allowed to feel safely as a kid?

9–12 YEARS: **Encouraging Reflection and Building Language**

* As your child starts asking more complex questions, are you noticing old discomfort or hesitancy in addressing conflict openly?
* What were you taught about being "respectful" or "obedient," and are those messages helping or hindering your parenting now?
* Are you able to say, "I don't know" or "Let's figure this out together," or does that feel threatening based on how you were raised?

- What kinds of conversations did your caregivers *never* have with you about emotions or conflict, and how can you offer that now?
- What's one story from your childhood about conflict that still sits in your body? How might you start to unpack it?

TEENAGERS: **Respecting Boundaries While Staying Emotionally Available**

- Did anyone in your family truly listen when you were a teen? How does that shape the way you respond to your teen now?
- How did your caregivers react when you challenged them, asked hard questions, or pushed back?
- Are there parts of you that still feel like the teen who wasn't heard, and how does that show up in parenting today?
- What were the spoken or unspoken rules about authority, control, or emotional expression in your family?
- What does it mean to hold space for your teen while healing the wounded teen inside yourself?

ADULT CHILDREN: **Revisiting Old Wounds and Repairing What Was Passed Down**

- Have you talked with your adult child about how conflict was modeled in your family when they were growing up?
- Do you recognize any old scripts being replayed between you and your adult child?
- Are there moments you can revisit together with gentleness and curiosity, not defensiveness?

* What's something you inherited around conflict that you're actively working to change, even now?
* What kind of legacy do you want to leave when it comes to emotional safety and repair?

Conflict in Parenthood: Fighting While Tired, Triggered, and Touched Out

There were times in my marriage when I surprised myself with how grounded I could stay during conflict, usually on the days when I'd had enough sleep, when the house was calm, and my nervous system wasn't already stretched thin. On those days, I could hear hard things without shutting down or getting defensive. I could respond instead of react. I could remember we were on the same team.

And then there were the other days. The ones where I'd seen too many clients back-to-back, when the kids needed me nonstop, and the noise of the day never really ended. On those days, it took almost nothing to set me off, a sigh, a comment, a look. My reaction was a mix of ADHD, exhaustion, overstimulation, and the feeling of carrying so much that no one else could see. When you're touched out, even gentle affection can feel like one more demand on a body already flooded with sensation. The brain interprets touch, sound, and emotion as the same kind of input, and when there's too much of it, everything starts to feel like noise.

Looking back, I can see that I wasn't the only one struggling. I'd take on too much and rarely ask for help, believing I had to hold it all together. But my ex also hadn't been taught to notice or respond to emotional needs in the same way I had. Many men are raised to focus on fixing rather than feeling, to stay composed instead of curious, and that left us speaking different emotional languages. It wasn't entirely his fault, and it wasn't mine, it was two people trying to love each other while working from mismatched blueprints. I could anticipate his needs easily, but he didn't always know how to anticipate mine, and over time that gap grew into distance. When stress hit, our patterns collided. I'd overfunction, trying to bridge the gap and pull us close again. He'd withdraw, needing space to think, which only made my anxiety spike higher. We'd end up stuck in a loop: me pursuing connection, him protecting himself. It's a common dynamic (anxious meets avoidant) and the harder each person tries to meet their own need, the further apart they drift. We tried to interrupt the cycle in small ways: taking breaks before the conversation spiraled, naming what was really happening underneath the irritation, reminding each other that tired doesn't mean unloving, and that needing space isn't rejection. Sometimes we managed to come back to each other gently; other times we couldn't.

Now, as co-parents, we're learning in our own ways how to do things differently. I'm learning to ask for help before I burn out, to pause before I overexplain, and to give myself permission to walk away before resentment sets in. He's learning to tune in, to notice, and to respond in ways that feel more connected. We're both trying to show up for our kids, and for ourselves, with more awareness than we had before.

Resource: *Burnout* by Emily and Amelia Nagoski is a compassionate and research-backed look at why so many of us are running on empty, especially caregivers and mothers, and what we actually need to restore ourselves. It helped me see that my reactivity is a signal, and that rest, nervous system regulation, and completing the stress cycle are the foundation for showing up in conflict the way I want to.

PRE-CHILD PLANNING: **Creating a Foundation Before Exhaustion Hits**

- How do you tend to act when you're emotionally spent: withdraw, snap, get quiet, or overfunction?
- Who in your life helps you notice when you're starting to run on empty?
- What are ways you can gently ask each other, "Do you need support or space right now?"
- Who can you call on for meals, childcare, or even just encouragement when things feel overwhelming?
- How can you talk about stress or resentment before it builds into something bigger?

DURING PREGNANCY: **When Sensory and Emotional Load Begins to Rise**

- What are you and your partner/co-parent needing more of lately: sleep, time alone, reassurance, flexibility?
- How can you check in on each other's stress levels without judgment?
- Are you making space for irritability without making it personal?
- Who in your community helps you feel regulated or held when things feel too much?
- How do you want to talk about hard days now, so it feels easier to do later?

POSTPARTUM: **Survival Mode, Tension, and Tenderness**

- What signs show you you're at your limit (tone of voice, body language, withdrawal)? Can you name those for each other gently?

* How do you ask for a break, or signal "I can't do this right now," without it becoming a fight?
* What helps each of you reset when you're overstimulated: movement, quiet, touch, talking?
* Are there ways others (a parent, friend, doula, neighbor) can step in so you can tag each other out?
* How can you protect your relationship from becoming the default outlet for your stress?

TODDLER YEARS: **Co-Regulating While Touched Out**

* When both you and your partner are depleted, how do you decide who gets a break and who steps in?
* Are there unspoken expectations you need to name (around bedtime, meltdowns, mornings)?
* What does support actually look like right now: physical help, words of affirmation, quiet, checking in?
* What behaviors from your toddler feel especially triggering, and can you talk about why?
* Who in your life can offer even small moments of relief or connection so you can reconnect as a team?

4–8 YEARS: **Making Stress and Tension Talkable**

* How do you and your partner/co-parent want to talk about conflict or big feelings in front of your kids?
* What small scripts can you use (e.g., "We're figuring something out together," "It's okay to have big feelings")?

* Are there moments when you each feel most reactive: mornings, meal prep, transitions? How can you buffer those?
* Who could you reach out to (a friend, a teacher, a counselor) if you need a sounding board or support?
* How do you each recharge, and are you honoring those differences in how you take space?

9–12 YEARS: **Modeling Regulation and Recovery**

* What are the early warning signs that one of you is burning out? How can you say, "I'm maxed out" without guilt?
* How are your kids responding to the emotional tone in the home? Are they withdrawing, acting out, or caretaking?
* Are you modeling that needing time alone, needing to talk, or needing help are all valid ways to handle stress?
* Who outside the home can help you process things so conflict doesn't always stay inside the family bubble?
* Are there rituals or routines that help you stay grounded and emotionally available (e.g., solo walks, check-ins, creative time)?

TEENAGERS: **Respecting Emotional Intensity and Independence**

* What helps each of you come back to a grounded state after conflict? Can you name that and ask for it?
* How do you repair with your teen when stress has spilled onto them? Do you offer real accountability?

* Are you asking your teen how they experience conflict in the home, and are you ready to hear the answer?
* When either of you needs space, how do you ask for it without making it feel like abandonment?
* Who in our lives can support you emotionally, outside of the relationship, so you're not relying only on each other?

ADULT CHILDREN: **Looking Back Without Shame**

* Have you ever talked openly about what stress looked like in your home when they were growing up?
* Can you name the ways your nervous system was overloaded without making it their job to understand or excuse it?
* Are there old patterns or stories they still carry about your anger, absence, or tension, and can you revisit those gently?
* What do you want to model now about stress, support, and repair, even as your roles shift?
* Who in your lives helps you reflect, grow, and stay accountable as parents of adult children?

Repair After Rupture: Finding Your Way Back to Each Other

There was a moment in my marriage when a small misunderstanding spiraled into silence that lasted most of the day. Not out of anger, but out of hurt and disconnection, the kind that makes it hard to reach for each other even when you want to. The argument itself wasn't what mattered; it was how easily we both slipped into old patterns. I shut down to protect myself, and he withdrew to avoid saying the wrong thing. The space between us grew heavy with everything unspoken. That kind of rupture is inevitable in any close relationship, especially in parenthood, when both partners are running on little sleep, high stress, and limited capacity.

You might know the feeling: one person says something in the wrong tone, the other gets defensive, and before you realize it, you're both reacting to old fears instead of what's in front of you. Maybe one of you goes quiet, maybe the other doubles down. The topic shifts, but the emotional distance stays. Repair doesn't always start with an apology or a perfectly timed conversation. Sometimes it starts with not making it worse, with staying kind even in silence, or choosing to pause instead of pressuring for resolution. Emotional repair is the process of gently finding your way back to safety with each other after a moment of rupture. It's what allows trust to rebuild over time.

If this sounds familiar, here are a few ways to approach repair when conflict leaves you both raw or disconnected: Pause before fixing. When emotions are high, nervous systems are activated. Give space for your bodies to settle before trying to talk things through, and actively learn what you need to come back into your body while you're taking space. Lead with ownership, not blame. Saying, "I can see how my reaction hurt you," opens a door faster than defending your intentions. Name what's underneath. Ruptures are rarely about dishes or tone, they're about feeling unseen, unheard, or unsupported. Naming that unmet need changes the conversation.

Stay soft. Repair happens in tone as much as in words. Staying gentle communicates safety, even if the words come later. Model repair for your kids. If you have an argument in front of your children, whether or not tension is high, but your kids can understand what's going on, don't just wait to repair behind closed doors. Even if initially that is what you do, do a "second round" in front of them so they can see that things got settled in a healthy way. When they see you apologize, take breaks, and come back together, they learn that love and accountability can coexist. When we approach conflict with curiosity instead of punishment, and softness instead of pride, we show our partners and our children that as long as we have good repair practices, conflict doesn't have to be scary or bad.

Resource: *Parenting from the Inside Out* by Daniel J. Siegel and Mary Hartzell unpacks how our own childhood experiences shape the way we parent, and, importantly, how rupture and repair are not only inevitable, but essential for building secure attachment. Siegel introduces the concept that you don't have to be a perfect parent, just a "good enough" one who returns, reflects, and repairs. The neuroscience and storytelling blend well to help parents understand how their children's developing brains respond to conflict and reconciliation, and how to use those moments to deepen connection rather than damage it.

PRE-CHILD PLANNING: **Learning What Repair Looks Like**

* What did repair look like in your family growing up, if it happened at all?
* Do you tend to avoid, rush through, or overfunction in repair?
* What phrases or gestures help you feel like someone is reaching back toward you?
* What kind of repair would you want your future child to witness between adults?
* Who in your life models repair well? What have they taught you?
* Can you and your partner identify a ritual or phrase that could symbolize reconnection (e.g.,

"Pause and try again," hand on shoulder, a walk, shared tea)?

- What would it take to offer repair to a friend or family member you've drifted from?

DURING PREGNANCY: **Building Small Rituals of Return**

- When emotions run high, what helps you come back to yourself?
- How do hormones, physical discomfort, or stress affect your ability to repair?
- Is there someone (partner, friend, care provider) who helps you regulate after conflict? How do they do that?
- What's your usual post-conflict pattern? Do you go quiet, over-apologize, or try to fix it quickly?
- Can you create a safe way to say "I want to reconnect" without diving into the problem right away?
- What's one repair phrase or ritual you want to practice now, so it feels accessible later?

POSTPARTUM: **Coming Back from the Edge**

- When both you and your partner are touched out or depleted, how can you signal the desire to reconnect without needing a full conversation?
- What does repair look like when privacy is limited and time is short? Can a soft word, a shared moment, or physical closeness be enough?
- What do you need to hear from your partner, doula, or support network when you're struggling to soften?
- Are there recurring patterns that need more than a quick repair—ones that deserve deeper reflection when capacity allows?

* Who else in your circle (therapist, friend, parent, or postpartum group) can help hold space for the emotional load and guide you back to connection?
* How do you offer yourself a pause when repair isn't immediate?

TODDLER YEARS: **Repair in Front of Little Eyes**

* How do you model "making things right" with your partner or co-parent when your toddler is nearby?
* What language can you use in front of your child that communicates reconnection (e.g., "That was hard for us, but we worked it out")?
* When you lose patience with your child, how do you come back to them gently and clearly?
* How do your child's reactions (clinginess, play changes, mood shifts) signal what they're absorbing emotionally?
* Who in your extended circle can support you in the hard moments, stepping in, giving space, reminding you to repair?

4–8 YEARS: **Teaching the Power of Repair**

* What stories, books, or routines could help your child understand that making mistakes is part of being human, and repair is part of love?
* When your child misbehaves or lashes out, how do you model an apology without shame?
* Do your child's teachers, caregivers, or family members practice repair, too? What messages are they getting outside the home?

* What phrases help your child feel safe after tension (e.g., "I love you even when we're mad," "We always come back to each other")?
* How do you include your child in repair between adults, so they know conflict is normal, and so is reconnection?

9–12 YEARS: **Encouraging Self-Reflection and Grace**

* Have you ever asked your child how they feel after tension in the home? Do they have a safe place to talk about it?
* How do you and your co-parent or support system model the *full cycle* of repair (accountability, listening, and re-attunement)?
* What's your child learning about taking responsibility and offering forgiveness?
* Who else helps your child reflect and feel emotionally safe (e.g., a grandparent, school counselor, mentor)?
* How do you invite your child into repair after you've been short, unfair, or distracted?

TEENAGERS: **Normalizing Imperfection and Accountability**

* Do your teens see you practicing humility and taking ownership of your part in conflict?
* What helps your teen feel like you're truly listening and not just "moving on"?
* How do you repair after moments where you crossed a boundary, misunderstood them, or minimized their experience?
* Can you name out loud when you've had a rupture and are working on repair, even if they don't respond immediately?

* What does emotional safety look like for your teen, and how can you cocreate that with them?
* Who else can help hold the emotional labor of parenting a teen: friends, therapists, coaches, mentors?

ADULT CHILDREN: **Healing Forward**

* Are there old wounds you've never returned to with your adult child or ones you've tried to, but haven't fully explored together?
* What have you learned about conflict and repair since they were young, and have you shared that with them?
* How do you create space for their truth, even if it's hard to hear?
* Are there small gestures you can offer now that say, "I see you, I'm listening, and I want to keep learning"?
* Can your repair be demonstrated through actions, not just words, showing up differently over time, asking consent to revisit the past, or practicing new dynamics in the present?
* What does it mean to leave a legacy of repair in your family, and who can support you in doing that?

Chapter 13

NEURODIVERGENT PARENTING: WHEN YOUR BRAINS WORK DIFFERENTLY

Parenting already asks a lot of us, emotionally, physically, mentally. For neurodivergent (ND) parents or those raising neurodivergent children, that load often includes invisible demands that many families don't see or fully understand. From sensory overload to executive dysfunction, social burnout to emotional intensity, parenting with or alongside neurodivergence can reshape how we show up in daily life, how we connect with our children, and how we care for ourselves.

This chapter invites you to explore what it means to parent in a world not built for all brains, and to find ways to meet your own needs and your child's with compassion, flexibility, and understanding. Whether neurodivergence lives in you, your child, or both, these conversations are about making space for what's real, not just ideal.

Understanding Neurodiversity in Family Life

Neurodiversity refers to the natural variation in how human brains function and experience the world. It includes ADHD, autism, OCD, dyslexia, dyspraxia, sensory processing differences, and more. These are not problems to be solved and gotten rid of; they're differences in wiring that affect attention, communication, learning, emotional regulation, and sensory experience, that we live with for our entire lives. For many neurodivergent parents, parenting can amplify traits they've spent their lives masking or managing. You might struggle with transitions, forget small tasks, or feel completely overwhelmed by noise, mess, or emotional demands. You might feel guilt or shame when your parenting doesn't look like what others expect. And yet, you're often also intuitive, deeply attuned to your child's needs, and profoundly creative in how you adapt.

If your child is neurodivergent, parenting may require rethinking everything you were taught about discipline, structure, and emotional expression. Neurodivergent kids often thrive in environments that emphasize flexibility, co-regulation, and sensory understanding, not rigid expectations. It's less about "getting them to behave" and more about helping them feel safe enough to be who they are.

Why Supporting Neurodivergent Families Matters

When we acknowledge neurodivergence in parenting, whether in the parent, the child, or both, we create space for a more realistic, respectful, and sustainable version of family life. We allow parents to ask, "What supports my nervous system?" instead of just "What am I doing wrong?" We shift away from shame and toward self-awareness.

We also help children see that their needs are not too much, and that being wired differently doesn't mean being broken. In families where neurodivergence is normalized, emotions are not punished, energy levels are not pathologized, and strategies are tailored instead of imposed. When we stop expecting ourselves to parent like everyone else, we can start parenting in ways that actually work for us. That's the gift of neurodivergent parenting: It invites us to slow down, listen closely, and build lives that honor our rhythms.

When You're the Neurodivergent Parent

My ex-husband and I were both diagnosed with ADHD in our mid-thirties, after decades of moving through life with this constant, confusing sense of *being different* but not quite knowing why. I've always been someone with what I now lovingly call "doom piles"—those little mountains of half-finished tasks or papers or laundry that I swear I'll get to but never do until the pressure is unbearable. I was the kid who could procrastinate an assignment for weeks and then hammer out a five-thousand-word A+ essay the night before. I'd forget my keys but remember every word of a conversation from three years ago. I stim by rubbing my fingers or picking at my skin (a self-soothing behavior common with ADHD that helps regulate sensory input or emotions). I talk fast, I interrupt, I lose things constantly, and I live in a near-constant loop of "Where did I just put that?" paired with "Wait, what was I doing again?" Time has always felt slippery to me; five minutes can vanish into hyperfocus while a whole hour can feel like it never happened. And the emotional side is just as real: shame after blurting something out, or tears from what seems like a "small" frustration to everyone else.

Before kids, I had just enough freedom and flexibility to make it work. My chaos had a rhythm and worked around my brain, so I built my life to match it. If I pulled an all-nighter to finish something, I could sleep in the next morning. If I misplaced my wallet, it only affected me. If I forgot to eat until 3 p.m., no one else went hungry. Becoming a parent stripped away all of that buffer. Suddenly there was no "catching up later." Diaper bags needed to be packed now. School pickup was at a fixed time whether I remembered or not. Meltdowns didn't pause because I'd lost track of my own regulation. There was too much to remember, too many moving parts, too much responsibility, too little sleep. The stakes felt impossibly high, my mask was cracking, and the margin for error was gone. Things started slipping, and I felt like I was failing, not just at being a mom and a partner, but at being a functioning adult. That's when I got formally assessed and diagnosed, as did my husband at the time. And let me tell you, while it didn't solve everything, it *did* explain a lot. We started medication, which helped, but it's only part of the puzzle. I've also had to rethink how my days are structured, how I manage transitions, how much stimulation I can handle, and how I speak to myself when something goes off the rails, because it still does. Even with meds, the mental load of parenting pushes every ADHD weak spot: mornings with multiple steps, never-ending laundry, the constant soundtrack of crying and toys clattering. It's like living with twelve open browser tabs and three of them start screaming at once.

One of the best gifts of diagnosis has been the relief of shared language. We both stopped thinking of ourselves as lazy or unreliable and started understanding our brains for what they are, wired differently. It reminds me of that time we drove ninety minutes to a festival only to realize, once we got there, that we had forgotten the *most important* thing: our daughter's formula. We had packed snacks, clothes, sunscreen, hats, but not her food. The mom guilt hit hard, but then I looked over and realized we *had* remembered my son's favorite little orange race car, which he was gripping like a treasure. That's ADHD in a nutshell: our attention isn't broken, it's uneven. We'll forget the obvious but cling to the tiny detail that lights up our brain. Parenting with ADHD, autism, OCD, or sensory processing differences means you're often working with a nervous system that's already overstretched. The mess, the noise, the unpredictability—they can all flood your capacity in seconds. For me, it's the combo of auditory sensitivity (every cry feels like an alarm bell) and working memory glitches (walking into the kitchen and forgetting why I'm there while a pot boils over). This subtopic is about noticing how your neurodivergence shows up in parenting, and more importantly, how to support yourself through it with structure and compassion. You don't need to have a formal diagnosis to be here.

Resource: The Neurodiversity Practice is a mental health collective offering therapy, consultation, and education rooted in a neurodiversity-affirming lens. Their work centers around reducing shame, honoring nervous system needs, and supporting individuals and families, especially parents navigating ADHD, autism, OCD, and other neurodivergent experiences. Learn more at: theneurodiversitypractice.com.

PRE-CHILD PLANNING: **Looking Back to Look Ahead**

* How was neurodivergent behavior (in yourself or others) viewed in your family growing up? Was it named, punished, misunderstood, or ignored?
* Were you celebrated for the ways you think differently, or shamed for being scattered, sensitive, distracted, or emotionally intense?

* What assumptions do you carry about what a "good parent" looks like, and how might those conflict with how you actually function?
* What parts of parenting do you expect might challenge your neurodivergent brain the most: sleep deprivation, executive functioning, noise, or emotional intensity?
* How do you want to explain your neurodivergence to your partner or support system so you can plan for moments when you might shut down or need help?
* What support tools (visual cues, shared task lists, body doubling, flexible routines) could reduce pressure *before* things fall apart?

DURING PREGNANCY: **Navigating Change with Self-Compassion**

* How is your ADHD/autism/OCD/sensory sensitivity showing up differently in pregnancy? Are you noticing more dysregulation, irritability, or overwhelm?
* Are you blaming yourself for symptoms like forgetfulness, mood swings, or exhaustion instead of recognizing them as part of how your brain and body are responding?
* How do you explain your neurodivergent needs (e.g., sensory accommodations, quiet time, step-by-step medical explanations) to your care team or birth partner?
* What systems might fall apart after the baby arrives, and how can you build in backup supports ahead of time?
* When you picture postpartum life, what would make daily routines feel manageable to *your* brain?

* Who in your life respects your processing style and won't try to "fix you" if you need to offload stress or ask for help?

POSTPARTUM: **When Old Systems Break Down**

* What parts of early parenting are overloading your nervous system the most: sensory input, decision fatigue, constant interruptions, or sleep deprivation?
* How do you speak to yourself in moments of forgetfulness or disorganization, and what would it sound like to respond with kindness instead?
* What executive function tasks (e.g., restocking diapers, managing appointments, remembering feed times) need delegation or external support?
* What does repair look like when your neurodivergent traits impact your parenting? Can you name it with your partner or baby and begin again?
* What moments make you feel like a *good enough* ND parent, even if they're small? How can you name and build on those?
* Who in your village and support team can help you celebrate small wins when all you can see is where you're behind?

TODDLER YEARS: **Regulation in Real Time**

* How does dysregulation show up in your parenting during chaotic or overstimulating moments?
* Are you modeling coping strategies that actually work for *your* nervous system: stimming, deep pressure, quiet alone time, scripting?

* Do you feel ashamed when you need more breaks than other parents, or can you name that as a valid part of your neurodivergent reality?
* What routines support both your toddler's needs and your regulation (e.g., visual schedules, structured flexibility, prep time before transitions)?
* How do you ask your co-parent or community for help without overexplaining or minimizing your need?
* Who understands what it's like to parent while ND and could help you feel less alone?

4–8 YEARS: **Growing Awareness and Language**

* What language can you use to talk to your child about your neurodivergence in a way that is honest, simple, and empowering?
* What does your child observe about how you handle emotions, noise, or unpredictability, and what do you want them to understand about it?
* Are you holding yourself to neurotypical parenting standards that don't actually serve you or your kids?
* How can you divide tasks with your partner in a way that honors how your brain works, not just what's "fair"?
* What helps you reset when you've snapped, shut down, or are overloaded, and how can you include your child in gentle repair?
* Who in your extended circle can reinforce neurodivergence as something *normal* and not shameful?

9–12 YEARS: **Building Understanding and Trust**

* How do you explain to your tween how your neurodivergence shows up at home, without oversharing or hiding it?
* What assumptions might they be making about your forgetfulness, reactivity, or lack of follow-through, and how can you help reframe that?
* How do you model self-regulation in age-appropriate ways when your system is overloaded? Do you name it or mask it?
* Are there parenting tasks (e.g., helping with school projects, scheduling, time management) where your ND traits impact follow-through, and how can you name that with compassion?
* What supports help you show up more consistently for them, and how do you model asking for that support openly?
* Who can you turn to when you need help parenting through the shame, overwhelm, or executive load of this stage?

TEENAGERS: **Practicing Honesty and Repair**

* How do you talk with your teen about the way your ADHD/autism/sensory traits impact how you show up emotionally, socially, or practically as a parent?
* What moments in parenting have been shaped by your neurodivergence, and have you named that openly or tried to pretend it wasn't happening?
* When you mess up due to overload, impulsivity, or shutdown, do you take responsibility in a way that models growth, not guilt?

- How can you explain to your teen that your regulation tools or limits might look different, but still reflect love and care?
- Are there emotional patterns or parenting habits (e.g., disorganization, talking too much, forgetting events) that you want to revisit together with humility?
- Who else in their life can help reinforce that it's okay to be human, imperfect, and still learning, especially as a neurodivergent parent?

ADULT CHILDREN: **Rewriting the Narrative Together**

- Have you ever named how your neurodivergence shaped their upbringing, whether through inconsistency, emotional intensity, or unique connection?
- Are there moments from their childhood that you now see differently through the lens of your diagnosis, and can you share that insight with accountability?
- Can you invite open conversation about how they experienced your parenting without centering guilt or shame?
- How do you show up now, as a still-neurodivergent, still-growing parent, and what kind of repair or re-attunement might be possible?
- What stories do you want to rewrite together, not to erase the past, but to better understand it?
- Who can support you in having these conversations, someone who understands neurodivergence and repair work in adult families?

Parenting a Neurodivergent Child

Whether there's a formal diagnosis or just a gut feeling you can't ignore, parenting a neurodivergent child can be incredibly rewarding, and unbelievably hard. It often means throwing out everything you thought you knew about what parenting was *supposed* to look like. These kids aren't misbehaving, they're not trying to be difficult, they're doing their best to cope with a world that often overwhelms their bodies, their brains, or their sense of safety. But when you're the one on the frontlines, it doesn't always feel that simple.

I've worked with neurodivergent kids in community mental health, and I've seen firsthand the resilience, creativity, and brilliance these kids hold, but also the pain and frustration that builds when they're constantly misunderstood. I've sat with parents who are completely burned out, grieving the idea of what they thought parenting would be like, and still waking up every day trying again with a child who doesn't fit the mold. Now, as a parent myself, I carry that perspective into my own home. My kids are still little, but I know enough to recognize the early signs. ADHD is highly heritable, and with both my kids' father and me diagnosed, it's likely that one or both of our children will have it, too. Honestly, my money is on my son right now. He has his own stims, his own sensory sensitivities. Loud, sudden sounds overwhelm him. Transitions are tough. Certain fabrics bother him. He's bright and funny and full of energy, but he gets flooded easily, and when he does, it's like watching someone unravel from the inside out. Sometimes it's the smallest thing, a sock seam, a change in routine, the wrong color cup, that tips him over. And once he's spiraling, it's not about the cup anymore, it's about his whole nervous system screaming "too much."

And when that happens, his dad and I have to be the ones to hold it all: his emotions, our responses, the judgmental stares in the grocery store, the intrusive thoughts about what this means long-term. It's bracing your body to carry him out of a crowded store while also fighting back the shame spiral in your own head: "Everyone is watching. They think I can't control my kid. Maybe they're right." There are moments when I feel like I'm failing him, like I should have seen the meltdown coming, or I should have handled it better, or I should have prepared differently. That's the cruel loop for parents like us. You're already maxed out, but your brain keeps replaying everything you "should have done." And then there are moments when I'm amazed by how clearly he knows what he needs, how he can say "too loud" or bury his face in his comfort object or demand space, and I think: *Maybe he's actually doing great. Maybe we both are, even if it's messy.*

Parenting a neurodivergent child often means being the interpreter between your child and the rest of the world. You're the one explaining why they can't tolerate birthday parties or why they need noise-canceling headphones at school or why their meltdown wasn't about the snack, it was about the day. It means emailing teachers about sensory breaks, practicing scripts before playdates, carrying noise-canceling headphones and comfort objects in your bag like other parents carry snacks. And at the same time, you're trying to manage your own inner world: the worry, the self-doubt, the pressure to get it right. It can be really lonely sometimes, especially when other parents compare their kids to yours or say things like, "He just needs more discipline," or "Have you tried cutting out red dye?" What they don't see is that you're not only helping your child regulate, you're also constantly educating the adults in the room—teachers, relatives, even strangers in checkout lines—so your kid can be understood instead of judged. This subtopic is about just that: the emotional complexity, the daily advocacy, the grief, the pride, the fierce love. It's about learning to see your child clearly, not through the lens of what they *should* be doing, but through the truth of who they are and what they need. It's about adapting your expectations, your self-talk, your idea of success, and remembering that you don't have to do it all alone.

PRE-CHILD PLANNING: **Exploring Your Beliefs and Support System**

* What would you need emotionally, practically, and financially if your child turned out to be neurodivergent?
* Do you carry fear around "labels" or diagnoses, and where does that come from?
* Growing up, what were the unspoken rules in your family about behavior, compliance, and "fitting in"?
* Can you talk with your partner honestly about how you might differ in how you respond to a child's dysregulation or sensitivity?
* Who in your lives (a friend, therapist, or educator) could be a safe sounding board if you start noticing signs of neurodivergence in your child?
* How do you want to show up for your child's needs if they conflict with what's socially accepted or "typical"?

DURING PREGNANCY: **Holding Possibility with Compassion**

* How would you advocate for your child if you suspected sensory issues, ADHD, or learning differences, and what support would you need to do that well?

* What anxieties do you have about parenting a child who is wired differently? Can you name them out loud without judgment?
* What ideas or expectations about "normal childhood" might you need to start loosening now?
* How would you want others to support *you* if you had a child whose needs were misunderstood by extended family or peers?
* What does your partner need to feel more confident if parenting looks more intense or layered than you imagined?

POSTPARTUM: **Reading Between the Lines**

* Are you interpreting your child's behaviors through a neurotypical lens, or are you getting curious about what's really going on?
* Are there patterns in your baby's reactions—sounds, lights, touch, routine—that could point to sensory sensitivity?
* What does your nervous system need when you're overstimulated *and* trying to help a baby who's overwhelmed, too?
* Can you share your observations with your partner without them feeling like you're overreacting, or vice versa?
* Who in your circle is good at validating and not minimizing, especially if early signs show up and you're not sure what it means yet?

TODDLER YEARS: **Honoring Difference Without Panic**

* When your toddler is melting down, are you trying to control the behavior or understand the *why* behind it?

* What signs of sensory sensitivity, emotional flooding, or rigidity are you starting to notice, and how do they land in your body?
* How do you want to talk to family members or childcare providers who say things like, "They just need more structure" or "She'll grow out of it"?
* What's one part of your day that feels hardest for your child, and what small shift could make it less overwhelming?
* Can your co-parent and you create a shared script when one of you is tapped out and the other needs to take over?
* Who in your extended network (a neighbor, friend, auntie) can show up for you without trying to fix or dismiss what's going on?

4–8 YEARS: **Reframing and Rebuilding**

* What does your child do or say when they're overwhelmed, and do you recognize it before it explodes?
* How do you talk to them about their needs in a way that's honest but not pathologizing (e.g., "Your brain works differently and that's okay")?
* Are you trying to get your child to act like other kids, or are you learning to see what works for *them*?
* How do you want to respond to schools or programs that offer "support" but don't feel safe or informed?
* What would it look like to let go of comparing, you as a parent, or them as a kid?
* Who can help you regulate *your own* nervous system when you're holding so much for theirs?

9–12 YEARS: **Listening More Deeply**

* What does your child wish adults (teachers, relatives, even you) understood about how their brain works?
* Are you showing up as their advocate, or are you unintentionally becoming their manager or fixer?
* What parts of their life light them up, and how can you make more space for those things even if they're not "productive"?
* How do you name the difference between dysregulation and disrespect when it comes to things like school refusal, impulsivity, or shut-downs?
* Can you ask your partner or a close friend to check in on *you*, not just the logistics of managing your child's needs?
* Who do you need on your "team" right now: therapists, specialists, family friends, neurodivergent adults, peer mentors?

TEENAGERS: **Repair, Resilience, and Respect**

* Have you talked to your teen directly about how you experience their neurodivergence at home without centering shame or authority?
* Are you treating their need for space, repetition, or routines as resistance or as part of how they function?
* How can you support their independence *without* making them mask or hide their traits to fit in?
* Can you talk to other parents of ND teens or young adults to get support for yourself, not just strategies for them?
* How do you keep modeling self-awareness and regulation, even when you don't get it right?

ADULT CHILDREN: **Revisiting the Narrative**

* Have you ever talked with your adult child about the possibility that their neurodivergence shaped your relationship and how you showed up as their parent?
* Are there moments you look back on now with a clearer understanding of what was actually going on for them, and can you name that out loud?
* Can you offer repair or validation for times they were told they were "too much" or "too sensitive," especially if you said those things, too?
* What do you want them to know about how hard you were trying, even if you didn't always have the language or tools back then?
* What parts of their identity, routines, or boundaries do you still struggle to understand or accept, and how can you work on that with support?
* Who can hold space with you as you reflect, not to shame you, but to help you keep learning how to be in a relationship with the adult they've become?

The Invisible Load: Showing Up Differently Without Burning Out

Being a neurodivergent parent means carrying a mental and sensory load that most people don't see and often can't even imagine. It's the medication refill you forgot until bedtime. The dinner ingredients you meant to pick up but didn't write down. The dishwasher you opened three times without remembering to actually unload it. It's the sharp sensory overload from the blender, the toddler screaming, and the tags in your shirt, all happening at once. It's the internal chaos of trying to do five things at once and finishing none of them. And the shame that follows when someone asks, "How could you forget *that*?"

For my co-parent and me, parenting with ADHD has made all of these things more visible. Before kids, I could survive on last-minute adrenaline. I'd live out of laundry baskets and rely on half-finished mental checklists I never told anyone about. My systems were invisible, and barely systems at all. But then I became a parent, and everything fell apart. The margin for error vanished. Forgetting something didn't just mean being late; it could mean missing an important appointment, forgetting medication, or not packing the one thing that helps my child feel safe in a chaotic world. So, we started building systems that worked *with* our brains instead of against them. We have a Skylight calendar in the kitchen that's become a central hub; it holds everything from doctor appointments to therapy, garbage days, chore rotations, and birthday party RSVPs. Seeing it all in one place has eased some of the pressure of the invisible load. We use recurring phone alarms and shared lists to keep us from forgetting the essentials. Routines live on paper, not in my head, and we've made our environment as regulation-friendly as we can.

There's dim lighting in most of our common areas, soft-close doors and drawers to cut down on sudden noise, and varied textures—soft pillows, plush rugs, a chunky knit blanket—scattered around the house to help us regulate through sensory input. We have a weighted blanket on the couch, a grounding bin full of tactile objects like smooth stones, putty, and fidgets, and noise-canceling headphones that I keep within reach when the sound levels get overwhelming. These tools let our nervous systems breathe so we can use them again.

Resource: *How to Keep House While Drowning* by KC Davis is written by a neurodivergent therapist and offers compassionate, shame-free guidance for managing care tasks when you're overwhelmed, burned out, or living with executive dysfunction. Davis's approach reframes housekeeping and parenting responsibilities and provides practical tools like the "Five Things Tidying" method, closing routines, and sensory-friendly systems. Her work is especially helpful for parents navigating ADHD or other neurodivergences while trying to show up for their families without burning out.

PRE-CHILD PLANNING: **Anticipating Support Before You Need It**

* What systems (calendars, medication reminders, shared checklists) have helped you function in the past, and what might you need to adapt for parenting?
* What were the safety blind spots you grew up with around neurodivergence (e.g., open flame, meds, forgetfulness), and how can you reduce those risks now?
* What tasks are you likely to forget or drop under stress, and how can your partner or support circle help fill those gaps without blame?
* What kind of prep do you need for overstimulation (earplugs, quiet breaks, visual reminders, and gentle "taps out")?
* What assumptions do you have about what "being prepared" looks like as a parent, and can you redefine that through the lens of how your brain works?

DURING PREGNANCY: **Managing Internal and External Overload**

* Are there specific sensory or cognitive changes showing up in pregnancy that are pushing your limits, and how are you adjusting for that?

- How can you set up external systems (Skylight calendar, alarms, whiteboards, recurring check-ins) now so you don't rely on memory alone?
- What are your early signs of overload: forgetfulness, agitation, frozen indecision? Who can help you name them in real time?
- What are small "automation" wins you can put in place now (e.g., auto-refills for prescriptions, shared grocery list apps)?
- How do you want to communicate your executive or sensory limits to your partner, doula, or care provider, especially if you "mask" in front of them (hide signs of overwhelm or try to appear more regulated than you feel)?

POSTPARTUM: **When Your Old Systems Fall Apart**

- What do you keep forgetting (bottles, meds, burp cloths, appointments), and how can you build consistent cues or backup plans to reduce panic?
- What kind of safety structures do you need in place for ADHD-related forgetfulness or overwhelm (e.g., phone alarms, visual to-do lists, childcare backup)?
- Where do you keep crashing, physically, emotionally, or mentally, and what system could make that load lighter or more predictable?
- Who can help you triage priorities when you can't think clearly, someone who won't shame you or push you to "just try harder"?
- What do you need to feel okay letting go of (e.g., meal planning, laundry folding, online responses), and who can you delegate that to?

TODDLER YEARS: **Living in Real-Time Dysregulation**

* What part of the day is consistently the hardest for your nervous system, and how can you scaffold it with external supports (e.g., prep bins, visual timers, meals on repeat)?
* When you feel like you're "dropping everything," what is actually missing: predictability, reminders, co-regulation, rest?
* What helps you reset after a meltdown (yours or your toddler's), and do you actually allow yourself that reset or just power through?
* What kind of safety cues (e.g., child locks, scheduled med checks, visual stop signs) reduce risk when you're mentally taxed?
* Can you talk to your partner or a friend about trading off "default parent" status during your most overloaded times of day?

4–8 YEARS: **Rebuilding Trust in Your Capacity**

* Where do you still beat yourself up for "failing" at routines, and can you shift the system instead of trying to fix yourself?
* What supports both your child's routine and yours (e.g., shared calendars, after-school bins, color-coded charts)?
* Are there parenting responsibilities you dread because of executive or sensory fatigue, and how can you adjust expectations or ask for help?
* What kind of prep or recovery does a birthday party, school event, or change in routine require for *your* regulation?
* Who helps you feel seen as a neurodivergent parent without over-advising or minimizing?

9–12 YEARS: **When the Mental Load Multiplies**

* What areas of parenting are hitting your executive functioning the hardest (e.g., school forms, project deadlines, social coordination), and how can you comanage those tasks?
* What systems could your tween and you cocreate that support both of you (e.g., daily check-ins, chore cards, shared alerts)?
* Can you model how you manage my limits: "My brain is full right now, can we talk about this after I check my list"?
* When you forget something important to your child, how do you repair and explain it without defensiveness?
* Are there assumptions you're holding (e.g., "I should just be able to do this") that keep you from asking for help?

TEENAGERS: **Modeling Realistic Functioning and Repair**

* Have you talked to your teen about how you track and manage things like appointments, bills, meals, meds, and how it's taken time to figure out what works?
* Are you still masking around your teen when you're overwhelmed, or are you willing to say, "I'm out of capacity right now, and that's okay"?
* What tasks do you keep forgetting or delaying (e.g., driver's ed paperwork, follow-ups, financial forms), and who can help you build scaffolding around them?
* Are you willing to show your teen what repair looks like after you forget, snap, or get lost in

your own overwhelm and not expect them to "be okay with it" right away?

* Who helps *you* feel less broken as a neurodivergent parent, especially when parenting a neurotypical teen who sees your struggles up close?

ADULT CHILDREN: **Revisiting and Revising Systems Together**

* Have you ever shared with a friend or therapist what it was like to parent while managing neurodivergence, and how much of that you kept hidden at the time?
* Are there systems or patterns you're still using that don't actually serve you—and could you open up to someone you trust about trying to change them, even now?
* Are there moments from your child's upbringing where you were dysregulated, overwhelmed, or forgetful that make more sense through a neurodivergent lens, and how can you hold that with accountability instead of shame?
* Who in your circle can sit with you in these reflections, someone who understands what it means to carry an invisible load through the most important years of raising a child?
* Can you ask for support (from a sibling, friend, or therapist) in revisiting some of the old stories you carry about parenting "failures" that may actually be symptoms, misunderstood needs, or misaligned expectations?

CONCLUSION

As I sit with everything this book holds, I keep thinking about what it's really trying to say underneath all the questions, stories, and reflections: that parenting is deeply personal, often overwhelming, and that it asks so much of us, not just logistically or physically, but emotionally, relationally, and generationally.

This was never meant to just be a book about parenting techniques or strategies. It was meant to be a book about what it means to try to show up for your child while still learning how to show up for yourself. It is about what happens when the stories you grew up with (about family, responsibility, identity, gender, love, safety) all come rushing to the surface as you move through sleepless nights, big feelings, and quiet moments that no one else sees.

We began by talking about voice, what it means to hear your own through the noise of family expectations, cultural norms, old coping strategies, and the loud opinions of people who may never have had to navigate the things you're facing. From there, we moved into the many layers that shape family life: how you relate to screens and technology, how money holds memories and emotion, how gender roles seep into your home even when you're trying hard to do things differently.

There were chapters that asked you to slow down and soften around mental health in the postpartum period, around intimacy and identity after kids, around those moments of disconnection that feel harder to name but are no less real. And there were chapters that asked for honesty, about how you feed your children and yourself, about safety and consent, about the kind of world you hope they inherit and the ways you model empathy, fairness, and repair.

Later in the book, we made space for what often lives in the background but shapes everything: the tensions that build over the holidays, the fights you wish you could rewind, the slow work of making things right after they've gone sideways. And for families whose experience of parenting doesn't look like the typical script, especially those navigating neurodivergence in themselves or their children, I wanted this book to say clearly: You're not doing it wrong just because you're doing it differently.

At the heart of it all is the idea that parenting is just as much about who you're raising as it is about who you're becoming. And you're allowed to "become" slowly, inconsistently, and in a way that doesn't always make sense until much later. Most people don't need more advice; they need space to name what's true. They need language for the things they've been carrying quietly. They need permission to not know what they're doing, and to still be doing something incredibly meaningful.

If this book gave you even a moment of pause—a question that helped you feel more grounded, a paragraph that made you exhale, a sense that someone out there gets how hard this is—then I'm grateful. That was the hope.

You don't need to leave this book changed. You don't need to have underlined every prompt or remembered every story. If anything, I hope you leave it feeling a little more connected to yourself. A little more able to notice what matters to you, not to everyone else, not to your upbringing, not to the internet, but to you.

Parenting will keep asking things of you. You will keep getting to know yourself in new ways. You'll lose your footing and find it again. You'll repair. You'll shift. You'll grow. You'll circle back. You'll love your kids so fiercely it hurts, and you'll still have days where you want to run away. That doesn't make you broken; it makes you human.

Thank you for letting these pages walk with you, for making space to reflect on the things that so often get pushed aside in the rush of daily life. I don't know your story, but I know that if you're here, you care deeply, and I hope that's something you can feel proud of.

With warmth, respect, and so much care for everything you're holding,

—Martina

ACKNOWLEDGMENTS

To my beautiful children: You have been my greatest teachers. Every day, you remind me of the importance of curiosity, love, and presence. You are the reason I strive to keep learning, healing, and showing up with as much honesty as I can. Thank you for the lessons you continue to teach me and for inspiring me to be better in all that I do.

To my dearest girlfriends, Ann, Aimee, Kaitlyn, Dominika (my amazing sister), Shannon, Grace, Dorota, and Amanda: Thank you for your vulnerability, care, laughter, and unwavering support. Your willingness to share your own truths about motherhood, relationships, and identity has given me both comfort and courage during some of the hardest moments of my life. You are the voices that keep me grounded and the hearts that make my world feel less lonely.

To my friends who have taught me about fatherhood, Kharan, Zach, Christopher, and Rob: Thank you for modeling what engaged, compassionate, emotionally attuned, and evolving fatherhood/partnership can look like. Your presence, reflection, and care have reminded me that the work of parenting and of healing is shared.

To my mom and dad: Thank you for teaching me resiliency, hard work, love, and tradition. You've shown me what it means to care deeply, to show up for family, and to stand by the people you love in hard times. I carry those lessons in everything I do.

To my ex-husband: Thank you for helping me create our beautiful children and for being part of the story that inspired this book. Much of what I've written came from trying to understand what wasn't working between us and what it means to rebuild from that place. Our story has changed shape in ways I never expected, and I'm still learning how to live with that. Even through the grief and distance, I see you growing in your own way, as a father and as a person, and I'm grateful that our children get to see that.

And to my incredible clients: Thank you for trusting me with your stories, your challenges, and your growth. Your openness, resilience, and vulnerability have deeply inspired me and helped shape the insights in this book. I am forever grateful for the honor of walking alongside you in your journey.

ABOUT THE AUTHOR

Martina Nova, MCP, RCC, is a Vancouver-based trauma-informed therapist and clinical director. She specializes in helping individuals and couples navigate anxiety, trauma, ADHD, and relationship patterns like people-pleasing. Over the past decade, she has worked in community mental health, health authorities, and private practice. As a first-generation Canadian, born in Slovakia and raised in Canada, Martina offers a culturally sensitive approach that honors each client's story. A mother of two and author of a therapy journal, she understands the complexity of balancing personal growth with life's many roles.

Other Ulysses Press Parenting Books

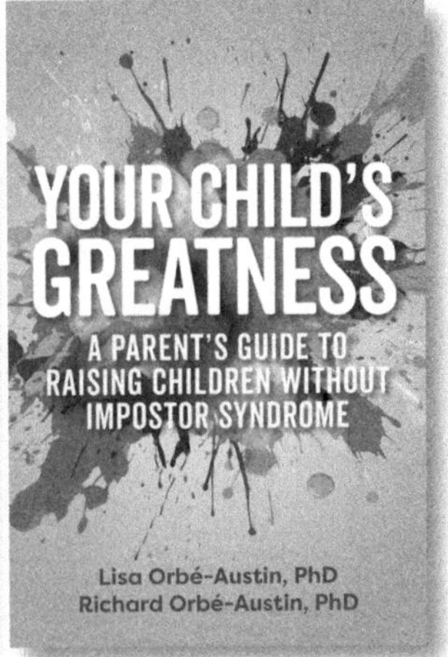

www.ulyssespress.com